I told you: I'm haunted. That's why I write what I write.

But the mournful call of an owl, so long ago, still echoes in everything I write. What I experienced that night is the same feeling I try to communicate in my writing. Not just "horror" or "terror," and I certainly don't go for the gross-out, but a deep ineffable feeling for the things the darkness can hide and that are beyond our understanding. I mean, when it comes to understanding life and death and the universe, we are all just frightened five-year-olds. I've said on occasion that because I don't sleep well, and have roaring nightmares that awaken me, often with a scream, sitting bolt-upright in bed bathed in sweat, maybe I'm trying to write something that will so unnerve my readers that they also might not be able to sleep, and when I'm awake in the middle of the night, I'll know—somewhere—someone—is also awake with me, and I don't feel so alone.

Is that a comforting thought?

It is for me.

Book List

Novels and Novellas
Beyond the Shroud
Cold River
Cold Whisper
Dark Silence
Dead Voices
Follow
Four Octobers
Ghost Light
Impulse
Little Brothers
Looking Glass
Moon Death
Moonbog
Moonwalker
Night Stone
Reunion
Shades of Night
The Mountain King
The White Room
The Wildman
Twilight Time
Unbroken
Winter Wake
The Body of Evidence Series (co-written with Christopher Golden)
Brain Trust
Burning Bones
Last Breath
Skin Deep
Throat Culture
Story Collections
Bedbugs
Glimpses: The Best Short Stories of Rick Hautala
Occasional Demons
Untcigahunk: The Complete Little Brothers

The Horror...
The Horror

An Autobiography

Rick Hautala

Crossroad Press

INTRODUCTION

In 1990, a young horror writer, and publisher of a magazine called *The Tome* stepped into another world. At NECON X I met rooms full of living legends. Robert McCammon, John Skipp, Craig Spector, Charlie Grant and F. Paul Wilson…and a very friendly guy with an odd resemblance to Martin Mull—Rick Hautala.

I'm not going to go into that experience in detail, but I am going to say that I was made to feel at home. I was drawn into conversations, treated as if I belonged. Rick, in particular, would talk to anyone. He always smiled, he had a million stories, and over the years, off-and-on, we remained friends.

He was one of the first authors who sat down and told me about the world of writing from the other side. Through successes, the problems when the mid-list crashed, his growing love of screenplays—he was candid, helpful, and full of enthusiasm. He was one of the most self-effacing writers I've ever encountered, with one of the biggest hearts, and he left a huge mark on the horror genre.

We are extremely proud to be bringing his works out in digital and helping to preserve his legacy—particularly with this short autobiography. Like that day I walked into NECON, you have a rare opportunity here. In these pages you'll meet one of the greats. Rick will be sorely missed, but his legacy lives on.

—David Niall Wilson

Prologue
"I 'Yam what I 'Yam"

You really want to read my autobiography?

I doubt it, but if you want a summary, the "short version," all you have to do is read the following quote from one of the best writers ever. I used it as the epigram for my collection of novellas, *Four Octobers*. It bears repeating:

> *"I want my place, my own place, my true place in the world, my proper sphere, my thing which Nature intended me to perform when she fashioned me thus awry, and which I have vainly sought all my life-time."*

Nathaniel Hawthorne wrote that something like two hundred years ago.

I especially like the "…when she fashioned me thus awry…" part.

So true for writers and artists in general, isn't it?

Everything that follows is mere commentary.

Chapter 1

"First Terrors"

You would think that growing up Finnish would be terrifying enough, but as far as I can see, I had a completely normal (at least to outward appearances) childhood. No drunk parents, no violent abuse beyond the usual "spankings" I got whenever I screwed up…which was often enough. I wasn't a wild kid, by any stretch of the imagination, but I crossed enough lines, and when I did and my folks found out, my father "corrected" me…strictly out of love, I'm sure…not like Jack Torrance in The Shining. When my father died, I was sad, and I miss both him and my mother on a daily basis. More on both of them later.

Although I was born in 1949 in Gloucester, Massachusetts, and lived the first five years of my life in Rockport, we moved to the house my father built in Pigeon Cove, diagonally across the road from the house my grandmother and grandfather lived in. My father built the house pretty much by himself, evenings and weekends, over—I have no idea how many years. He was an electrical engineer, but besides the wiring, he also did the framing, masonry, plumbing, finish work…pretty much everything. One of my earliest memories (but certainly not the first—more on that later, too) was mixing cement for the granite stone foundation. We have pictures of "Little Ricky" (Don't *ever* call me that!) mixing cement and carrying a hod full of bricks. Years later, after grad school, I worked as a mason's tender for a while. I never liked the work.

As "normal" as my childhood was, it was a different story

when it comes to my imagination. This is where we may begin to understand why I write what I write.

I grew up—and remain—scared.

Scared of what? (You may ask.)

The answer is simple enough: I was scared of both life and death.

In trying to figure out why I write horror…and not just "horror" since most of my novels are ghost stories…I wonder—often—why I feel so damned haunted…especially because I came from a loving, warm home with loving (if strict) Finnish Lutheran parents, a kind sister two years older than I, and a bully of a brother one year my elder. Maybe he's the reason I turned out warped. More on that later (perhaps…this shouldn't be a therapy session).

Okay, so we can agree that, for better or worse, for whatever reasons, I'm haunted.

Haunted by what? (You may ask.)

I'm not sure. I mean, I could make a list of the things that frighten, unnerve and terrify me, but it's deeper than that. Maybe writing this essay will help me focus on the reason with some clarity, but I have to tell you that I have increasingly come to believe that self-analysis isn't necessarily good for a writer. It's a given that most (maybe all?) writers are warped. I tell people in interviews and the few public lectures I've given that writing is a disease because its source is "dis-ease."

Am I saying I'm diseased?

Well, yeah. I guess so. More on that later, too.

So back to my childhood. Maybe it's significant that my first clear memory is an incident where I was absolutely, totally terrified. It happened like this. We were coming home from a visit to my grandmother's house (in Lanesville, Massachusetts, where my mother grew up) to the home I lived in for the first five years of my life. So I was no more than five years old...probably younger. It was dark. I mean, *really* dark. The house was a fair distance from the main road, and it was the only house on the dead-end street, so it was quite isolated...surrounded by woods and a large quarry that still supplies Rockport with its drinking water.

When we got out of the car, I heard a sound. If I describe it to you now simply as "An owl, hooting in the dark woods," you won't begin to appreciate how frightening that sound was. A low, whistling hoot, faint with distance, wafted through the night. It, in fact, seemed to be *part* of the night.

I was petrified. I remember I started crying. With tears streaming down my face, I asked my parents what that sound was. Someone—probably my mother—calmly explained that it was "just an owl."

Just an owl!

The sad, lonely notes drifting to my ears from the dark wood were all but supernatural in their effect. They reached to the deepest levels I could have had at five years old, and something was awakened in me for the first time.

And not the last.

That sound could have come from a lost and lonely ghost, crying in the night for the life it had lost...it could have been a demon, wailing in the dark, calling to other demons or trying to lure an unsuspecting human deeper into the woods...it could have been anything, but it was definitely *not* "just an owl."

So is that why I write horror? That terrifying experience... an experience for which—to my mind, anyway—had no rational, reasonable explanation…opened a door in my—what?

My mind?

My imagination?

My soul?

All of the above?

Perhaps, but there's one more element to this story that may also explain why I write what I write. My older brother, Bob. When I heard the owl hooting and reacted in such panic and started crying, he started laughing at me. The humiliation I felt for reacting as I did was devastating…especially to a dopey little kid who had never heard an owl hooting in the night. Even now, when I hear an owl calling, I am overcome with a soul-deep awe.

This wasn't the first or last time my brother tormented and mocked me. There's a reason I wrote a novel titled *Little Brothers*.

Like I said, though, my brother was—I can't sugarcoat it— he was a bully through and through. He lived to pick on me, always beating me up and making me cry. We squabbled continuously, and, I'm sure, drove my mother nuts with our endless fighting. My sister would lecture us, telling us we should be kind and loving. And then, from my mother, we heard the words a lot of people in my generation heard and reacted to with sheer terror: "Wait until your father gets home." When my father did come home, we straightened up because he didn't hesitate to "give us a lickin'." I'm sure it would be construed as child abuse now, but when I was a kid, my friends and I all got "lickin's." It's just the way it was.

My brother's laughter at me that night I first heard an owl only made the terror deeper…stronger. And yes, his laughter increased my lifelong resentment for my brother who has to this day done everything he can to torment and abuse me, emotionally, if not longer physically.

Were there other terrors in my early life?

Oh yeah. I had (and still have) nightmares several times a week.

I told you: I'm haunted. That's why I write what I write.

But the mournful call of an owl, so long ago, still echoes in everything I write. What I experienced that night is the same feeling I try to communicate in my writing. Not just "horror" or "terror," and I certainly don't go for the gross-out, but a deep ineffable feeling for the things the darkness can hide and that are beyond our understanding. I mean, when it comes to understanding life and death and the universe, we are all just frightened five-year-olds. I've said on occasion that because I don't sleep well, and have roaring nightmares that awaken me, often with a scream, sitting bolt-upright in bed bathed in sweat, maybe I'm trying to write something that will so unnerve my readers that they also might not be able to sleep, and when I'm awake in the middle of the night, I'll know—somewhere—someone—is also awake with me, and I don't feel so alone.

Is that a comforting thought?

It is for me.

Chapter 2

"More Frights"

I will never poke a dead animal with a stick.

Let's get that straight right away.

I am not someone who enjoys the gruesome, bloody, or violent in anything…not in fiction and not in the world. Some people might even say I am squeamish. Holly and my sons take a bit of delight when, occasionally, at mealtime someone raises a fairly disgusting topic. They take pleasure and even laugh at how I can't listen to gross stuff when I'm eating.

I'm not saying I'll throw up. I've seen my share of violent, gruesome, gory movies and I've read books high on the gag factor. I can sit through them (as long as I'm not eating). But when it comes to "horror," I fall squarely on the "Charlie Grant" side of the spectrum. I like my horror "quiet" and "subtle" and "unnerving," rather than bloody. I'm not saying the gruesome doesn't have its place or that "my" type of horror is superior. I'm just saying what I prefer and what I try to do. (Emphasis on the "try.")

But let's talk movie frights for a while because it wasn't just owls hooting in the woods that scared me.

I can't remember the year, and even a moment of research on the Internet would give me the right answer, but I was around ten years old when I saw my first horror movie. It was *Rodan*, and I saw it in the theater when it first ran. So you can figure out the year, subtract 1949 (the year I was born) from it, and you'll know how old I was when this happened. I prefer to "imagine"

I was nine or ten years old.

My brother and a friend of ours—John Halman, another Finn—went to see the movie. There was no "parental advisory" board back then, but my mother made it absolutely clear that she didn't want me or my brother watching such things because they would give us nightmares.

(Interesting concept: "Give" us nightmares—like a nightmare is a gift you receive. I like that!)

Around the time I was ten something else happened. There was this new TV show called *The Twilight Zone*, but more on that later because of the three or four people you can blame for me becoming the writer I am, Rod Serling is at the top of the list.

Back to *Rodan*.

My brother, his friend, and I took the bus to the Strand Theater in Gloucester, paid for our tickets (Damned if I can remember how much. Probably a quarter or so), went in, and sat down.

Other than a Disney cartoon or two, this was one of my first experiences in a movie theater, and not too long into the film, I began to be upset...Did I say "upset?" I mean scared... frightened, and it wasn't long before I was terrified and—you guessed it—I started to cry. I cried so much I had to leave the theater. My brother and his friend John came with me. Thank God they didn't turn me loose alone on the streets. But, my brother, once again, began to make fun of me because I was a "scaredy cat." (That was the extent of our insults back then. It was a kinder, gentler time.)

My brother was relentless in his teasing, and in at least one way, I can't say as I blamed him. He did want to see the entire movie, but his numb little brother couldn't handle it, so he and his friend who were a whole year older than me lost out.

That wasn't the only movie that scared the bejesus out of me, but it was the only one I got so scared watching I had to leave. Years later, when people were throwing up and having to leave *The Exorcist*, I actually found myself laughing at how absurd the movie was...on some level.

My next movie was *The Blob*—the original, not the remake. I had trouble with this one, too—my mother was right, it "gave" me nightmares—but I was already predisposed to nightmares, anyway. So I sat through it. Again, a little research will turn up the year *The Blob* was released, so I could figure out how old I was.

I enjoyed the creepy feelings this movie gave me, and I found other scary movie experiences more pleasant than terrifying.

Chapter 3
"Humor and Horror"

Then there were girls.

I discovered girls early. My "first love" was a girl named Sue Crowell. I was five years old. I know that because we were living in the house in Rockport, and Sue lived not too far away, on Landmark Lane. We kind of lost touch over the years, through elementary school, after I moved to Pigeon Cove; but in junior high, when all us "Cove-ahs" went to junior high and high school in Rockport, Sue and I reconnected. I think we even went steady for a while. I gave her a tie clip to wear. How quaint!

But after Sue, there were several other girls. When I was in junior high, one of the things we did to "date" was arrange to meet our steadies at the Strand Theater. (Sadly, the Strand went out of business. The building is now a liquor store. Sign of the times.) I remember that the first movie I went to with a girl was *The Premature Burial* with Vincent Price. I can't remember who I went with. In junior high, we changed girlfriends almost as frequently as we changed socks. My "date" might have been Jackie Tuck, who, like Sue Crowell, is happily married today. This would have been a year or so before Jackie slapped me across the face in Roy Moore's math class.

Now, I have to admit that our rationale for going to a scary movie was simple. We were hoping the girls we were with would get so scared during the movie that they would cuddle closer and closer to us as the tension built. My friends and I, I'm sure, had our own tensions building in our pants. We hoped against hope that we would maybe even get to put an arm around our girl's shoulders and—if we were *really, really* brave—maybe even kiss her.

No French kissing and certainly no "copping a feel," much less rainbow parties like junior high kids have today. All we wanted was to touch a real live girl, and getting her to a horror movie seemed like the easiest way to get her to cuddle.

I had a problem, though.

I was more frightened by the movie than the girl I was with.

Laugh all you want. It's a sad truth. I was petrified, and if I did get to hug and maybe even kiss my date, I forgot. But the memory of how frightened I was during that movie is almost as sharp today as it was back then.

This wasn't the last time I messed around with a girl in the movies. I got better at it. But don't fret, I'm not about to go X-rated on you. I do, however, have a funny little story from when I was in college in the Sixties.

(For the record: I was an undergraduate at U Maine Orono from 1966 to January 1971. I started work on my Master's in English in 1971 and got my degree in 1974.)

Back to the story: Dateless, as was often the case for me during my college years, I went with some friends to a free screening of *Psycho* on campus. As it happened, a girl I was interested in sat directly in front of me with some of her friends. I was dying to talk to her and maybe even work up the courage to ask her out for coffee or something after the show. (We all know what any college guy means by "or something.")

During a particularly tense scene in the movie…it might have been the famous shower scene…I don't remember…I got what I thought was a brilliant idea. I leaned forward and very lightly brushed my fingertips across the back of the girl's neck. She jumped. She shrieked. She stood up and spun around to glare at me, and in front of the entire audience, screamed, "You ASShole!"

We never dated.

But I had learned something valuable that served me in later years. I learned that people often use humor as a defense against "horror" and fear. I mean, why not laugh? Someone famous once said: "If you don't laugh, you'll cry; I prefer the former. Less cleanup," or words to that effect. I think it might have been Kurt Vonnegut, God rest.

Okay, so my first attempt at mixing humor with horror didn't work out as well as I had hoped. But it was a start, crude though it was.

Somewhere between these two events (having to leave *Rodan* and getting yelled at by a beautiful girl in a crowded theater) there was another movie that terrified me. Research, again, would give me the exact date and my age, but does it really matter?

The movie was the Disney film Darby O'Gill and the Little People.

Do you remember it? This was one of, if not *the,* first movie with Sean Connery in it. But Connery—as good as he was a few years later in the Bond movies—wasn't terrifying.

It was the *banshee.*

If you've seen the movie, you damned sure remember the *banshee.* If you haven't seen it, I would suggest that, even as an adult, you find a copy of this movie and watch it. Besides having one of the most frightening supernatural elements out there, it has—to my way of thinking—an almost perfectly structured story.

But the *banshee*. I won't ruin the experience for anyone who hasn't seen the movie, but it is without doubt the most frightened, the most unnerved, I have ever been in a movie. Maybe I was so scared because I was so young. Maybe what got me was the simply terrifying concept that when you hear a banshee's wail, you know someone in your family will die soon and *it might be you!* Maybe it was the coffin-like interior of the Death Coach.

I don't know.

All I know is, I want to recapture in my own writing that stark, nameless dread I felt watching that scene in *Darby O'Gill and the Little People*. I'm glad my brother wasn't there to tease me about it. Maybe he was, and I was so used to it I don't remember. He does, to this day, tease me for crying at the end of *Lassie, Come Home*, but that only proves he has no heart.

Chapter 4
"Your Next Stop"

So why do I write what I write and not, say, westerns or romances or (Heaven forfend!) "lit'ry" novels?

The answer is probably buried (and not very deeply) in the list of authors I read and was impressed by when I was growing up. There are only a few who are absolute landmarks. In no particular order, they are: Edgar Rice Burroughs, Ray Bradbury, Rod Serling (both when I had to sneak to watch the show and when I read the anthologies he compiled), Alfred Hitchcock collections, Nathaniel Hawthorne, and—yes, above all—William Shakespeare. (Come on! Take the ghost out of *Hamlet* or the witches out of *Macbeth*, and you have no story!)

Of course there are many other writers who influenced me later in life. Can you say Kurt Vonnegut, James Lee Burke, and Stephen King?

I knew you could.

If I start naming names, though, I know I'll forget (and possibly insult) dozens of other writers I consider mentors, and in many fortunate cases, good friends.

But let's start with good old Rod Serling and *The Twilight Zone.*

Forget about the "social consciousness" and the surprises and jolts to the system in any *Twilight Zone* story. Who doesn't remember the gremlin peering in the airplane window at William Shatner in Richard Matheson's classic episode? Serling's show, whether he wrote the episode or not, displayed a mastery of "hiding" social commentary. If you didn't see what, say, "The Monsters are Due on Maple Street" was saying about us as a species, then you're riding in the wrong part of the hearse.

But Serling did something more profound than "social commentary," at least as far as I was concerned as an aspiring writer. Truth to tell, I'm not sure I was aspiring to be a writer then. Later on, I did aspire. I'll tell you what really opened the door for me.

Serling made being a writer look totally fucking *cool.*

Come on. Admit it.

What was my sense of a writer before *Twilight Zone*? For a long time, it was what are now called "Dead White Guys"— Hawthorne, Poe, Hemingway, Faulkner, you know …all those writers…all of them were, to me, anyway, aloof…distant… refined…miles away from the common. And then—here comes Rod Serling. The TV didn't show how short he really was, but here's this cool looking guy who was smoking a cigarette while he introduced the evening's episode, and he was talking *passionately* about story and character and meaning.

Rod Serling was a genius as well as an amazingly prolific storyteller.

Sure, not every TZ show was a classic, but when you consider the pressure-cooker circumstances under which he produced *Twilight Zone*, you have to be astounded. The Beatles didn't do *Sgt. Pepper's* every time out either.

My mother, of course, wouldn't let me watch the show when it first ran, so I didn't see all the episodes in their original run. I had to sneak watching the show, and I saw enough to know this show and these stories and this guy Serling were *cool*! I have no doubt that the seed was planted early in my mind that I wanted to be a "cool" writer like that guy on *Twilight Zone.*

What got to me most in *Twilight Zone*—just like an owl, hooting in the night-shadowed depths of the forest—was the tone of so many of the TZ shows, struck with sentimentality... nostalgia...wistful longing...and chances lost and gone.

"Of all sad words of tongue or pen,
The saddest are these: 'It might have been.'"

Okay, so Rod Serling didn't write those lines, and you may be stunned that I've actually quoted poetry in this piece, but in the end—and in what was the beginning for me as writer—"being cool" and "nostalgia" were the most important lessons I learned during my time in..."The Twilight Zone."

Chapter 5

"Swinging Through the Trees"

I think we're clear now that I was…not really a "geek" in junior high school. I don't think the term had been invented yet. Maybe it had, in California, and like all good things took its time coming to the East Coast. But I was definitely…different when I was a kid. I might say I was the "black sheep" of the family. (What writer isn't, other than Owen King and Joe Hill?)

I wasn't a spaz, but I wasn't really athletic.

I played baseball, both Little League and pickup games with friends.

In high school, I ran track. I did the pole vault. (Best height: 10' 6"…not bad for back then), and I ran the high hurdles.

Here's a sad story for you: In individual team meets during my senior year, I ran against and beat everyone in all the schools in our (admittedly small) conference. Then, when we had the big conference meet, I was hoping to do it all again and win first place in the states. Because there were so many runners, we ran on the field instead of the track. After clearing the first hurdle, when my right foot came down, one of my spikes hit a rock, and I went face down on the ground…I came in last. Life lesson, there, folks!

I also liked to draw and paint, but I wasn't nearly as good as a handful of friends in school—Frank Sheldon and Alan Crane, especially.

I liked to read, but the books I chose to read were…odd, according to my English teachers.

I had always been a compulsive reader. My mother, God rest, encouraged me to read and, I think, was aware that I was the "dreamer" of her children. She always enrolled me in some book club or other. First there was the "First Book" series and then the "Landmark" series. These were educational books, usually dealing with science, nature, or history. Later, when I was in college, she enrolled me in the Time Reading Program, which published great—but unappreciated—books of fiction and non-fiction. The text editor was a man named Jerry Korn, who later went on to edit many of the famous Time-Life series of books. Years later, I served for two years on the Maine Arts Commission with Jerry.

But back in the seventh grade, I was awkward with girls, growing a nice little crop of pimples on my chin and forehead, and trying my best to find *some* way to express the thoughts and feelings of guilt and sadness and nostalgia I had churning inside, that seemed to have no outlet.

Why did I feel sad and guilty and nostalgic?

I have no idea.

It's just the way I was (and am) wired.

I also suffered (and still do) from a terrible sense of inferiority. I know where this comes from. It's from having a workaholic father (God rest) and an older brother who delighted in both putting me down and beating me up. The ups and downs of sibling rivalry.

It's my low self-esteem I want to address right now. You see, one thing I am sure of is that writing is an all but impossible job if you want to feel a sense of accomplishment. If you're doing it correctly, you are *never done!* Even when you finish a new story or novel or screenplay, you *have to* get on to the next piece of work. There's a line from a movie I'll never be able to identify, but it says "In a job like yours, even when you think you're finished, there's always one more thing to do."

That's the curse of being a writer, but when I was a kid, that's also how I felt about life.

My older sister and brother far excelled me in scholastics, athletics, and "social life" (as in: they had one, and I didn't). I can't tell you how many times a teacher said to me, "You're not half the student your brother and sister are." If that sounds familiar to you, you're probably a writer or artist of some type, too.

So what did I do?

Sure, I had a "normal" childhood, at least outwardly, but I was a dreamer. I lived in an imaginary world, and when toys had to be put away like all things of childhood I needed something to fill the void. Fortunately, I found books. I was a voracious reader, but I found myself drawn to—and reading—books that most of my teachers despised.

I say "most" because there was this one teacher…Fred Ives. He was my seventh grade social studies teacher, and once he moved up to the high school, my history teacher. One day, I was up at a bookcase, filled with books for "extra" reading. Mr. Ives came up to me and asked if I *really* had all my work done. I, of course, immediately panicked. Since I was *not* half the student my sister and brother were, I took the implied criticism and asked, "Am I missing any homework?"

Mr. Ives chuckled and said that he wanted to lend me a book. He told me I could not laugh or prejudge the book based on any movies I may have seen, that the book (the first in a series) was *far* better than any of the movies based on said series.

Intrigued now (and relieved that I wasn't in trouble for not doing all of my required work), I said something intelligent like, "Ahh…yeah…okay."

He went to his desk and got a dusty red book, no book jacket and handed me a hardbound copy of *Tarzan of the Apes.*

I have to admit that I wanted to laugh—I had seen a few of the lame movies—but I recognized even then that Mr. Ives must have seen something in me that indicated I would respond to an action adventure of the kind Edgar Rice Burroughs wrote. (Andrew Stanton, the writer/producer of *Finding Nemo* and *Wall-E* graduated from my high school years after I'd been there, and while I don't know if Andrew had Mr. Ives hand him a Burroughs book, I wonder why Stanton's next project is *John Carter of Mars*).

I read the first Tarzan book which, if you've read it, you know ends on a cliffhanger. When I returned the book, Mr. Ives was smiling as he said, "Do you want the next one?"

Did I?

You bet!

And it was Fred Ives, history teacher in Rockport, Massachusetts, who opened my eyes to fantastic fiction far beyond the books I'd been reading up to that point. Fortunately it was only a few years later that Ace Books started publishing paperback editions of Burroughs's novels—Tarzan, Barsoom, Amtor, Pellucidar, et al—in small, forty-cent editions. You know the books—the ones with the amazing Frazetta and Roy Krenkle covers and title page illustrations.

I bought and read (sometimes in a single sitting) every single Burroughs book they published. I bought two copies, in fact: one for reading and one "to save" in pristine condition. On summer days, I would sit under a tree—or sometimes perch on a branch twenty or so feet above the ground—and read Burroughs books.

My brother teased me about it, but what better place to read Tarzan than in a tree? Sure, Rockport wasn't Africa, but in my mind it was.

Then one day a few years later, someone in high school—a friend of mine, Frank Sheldon—showed me an issue of a science fiction magazine called *Analog* because he, like me, was a Burroughs freak. This particular issue had a review of some of the Ace Burroughs editions, so I bought the issue and then just happened to read a few of the other stories in the magazine.

Needless to say: "Wow!"

Not long after that, Ace Books came out with their (apparently pirated) editions of Tolkien's *Lord of the Rings* trilogy. Remember the ones with the blue, yellow and red covers? I read those in—it must have been 1963 or so. Again, a little research would give me the exact year, but I'm winging this whole thing, so I'll keep guessing.

That was it. I was gone—an addicted science fiction, fantasy, horror reader who devoured books upon which my English teachers frowned.

But I didn't care. I was beginning to live a life of the imagination and dreams, and—yes, when I was a kid, I sat in my dark bedroom looking out my window and up at the moon and stars, and wishing...*praying* that I could be transported to another planet and live a life filled with adventure like John Carter.

Instead, I grew up to be a writer.

How is *that* fair?

Chapter 6

"Bradbury Summer"

Okay, so it wasn't all imagination, dreams, fears and nightmares, but there was one writer who combined all of these and then some: Ray Bradbury.

I was sneaking watching *The Twilight Zone* and later reading Burroughs and Tolkien and *Analog*, but at some point I encountered Bradbury's work and realized, among other things, that this man could *write*! For the first time, I think, I didn't read for the story; I also read for the style…the voice…the poetry of the written word. I still value story above all else, but Bradbury was the first author I read who had a style—a tone…a mood—that I noticed.

And it hit me like the proverbial ton of bricks. Even today, I could show you the exact *spot* where I was sitting when I read *The Martian Chronicles* for the first time. It was at one of the granite quarries where I used to swim as a kid.

Here's where my "normal-at-least-to-outward-appearances" childhood and the writer I eventually became originated.

Until I was in high school, I didn't have a job except on weekends, when I helped my father—who was a land surveyor—doing fieldwork. Since I was the younger son, I was, of course, the "backsight man," which meant I stood there, bored out of my ever-lovin' mind while I held a plumb bob or other marker at the position where my father had previously set his transit and had now moved ahead, sighting either ahead to my brother or another helper.

Of course I always brought a book with me, and my father who was nothing if not a hard-headed, practical Finn would tell me to put the book down and concentrate on my "damn job." Since my "damn job" required standing around doing absolutely nothing for long stretches of time, I decided I *didn't* want to concentrate on it, so I continued to read, trying to hide the book from my father. I think he knew what I was doing, and I'm sure—to his dying day—that he did not "get" me.

I don't blame my father for being the practical workaholic he was. He graduated high school in June of 1929, so right around the time he was starting college at Northeastern, studying Electrical Engineering, the Great Depression hit. Timing is everything. My father's father, who—like my mother's father—was a quarry man, lost his job, and from then until the day my grandfather died, my father supported his mother and father as well as his own family with a wife and three kids once we came along.

He was a hard worker, my dad. He was the Town Engineer for Rockport and, later, worked for the city of Gloucester until he quit to do survey work full time. And I mean *full time*. We're talking eighty hours a week minimum. I don't remember him ever *not* working when he was awake except other than meal times. Even when he was in his eighties and early nineties, he barely slowed down. More than anyone else, he taught me that: "In a job like yours, even when you think you're finished, there's always one more thing to do." Today, when I am trying to relax and forget—at least for a while—whatever I'm currently writing, I (and the love of my life, Holly—Thank you, NECon!) have to remind myself to tell my father to be quiet.

We never took family vacations, although when we were

young, on sunny summer days, my mother would take us to the family granite quarry (We called it "going to the pit.") to swim and work on our future cases of skin cancer. Later, once I was too old to go with my mother, I used to hang out with friends—and try to meet girls—at the beach or at a quarry called "Steel Derrick."

My mother was an amazing woman because I think she was the first person to realize I was a dreamer...an imaginative boy who in many ways did not, and constitutionally *could not* fit into the "normal" (whatever the hell *that* means) work-a-day world. One clear memory I have from early childhood right through adulthood when I would come home to visit is of my mother asking me first thing in the morning not "How did you sleep?", but rather "What did you dream?"

What a question!

What did you dream?

She taught me—perhaps without realizing it—just how important dreams are to ...well, everyone, but especially to someone who values imagination, with all its light and dark facets.

Now you may think I've drifted off course here, but I haven't. I remember that I was talking about Bradbury. I merely want to emphasize again that I was not some socially awkward, frightened, bordering on paranoid kid. Sure, I had a bully of a brother, a taskmaster of a father, and a head full of rational and irrational fears that I couldn't talk about with anybody, but I also had a handful of good friends. We ran around the neighborhood and raised our own kinds of hell, doing lots of crazy things that today, no doubt, would get us arrested and slapped with mandatory community service and psychological counseling. But back then, it was what kids did.

We did all the things kids did before video games and the Internet. We played kickball in the street, hide 'n' seek, baseball; we ice skated and went sliding (we called it "sledding"). We swam in the Atlantic Ocean and in fresh water granite quarries; we set off firecrackers (usually in a neighbor's mailbox or on their rooftop), built "huts" in the woods, explored the Indian Caves nearby, picked blueberries and blackberries, met up with girls and tried to kiss them and, later, cop a feel...all that stuff, that magical stuff that Bradbury captured so well in his writing (well, maybe not the "copping a feel" part). Bradbury, along with echoes from Rod Serling's *Twilight Zone* combined with Burroughs and Tolkien, made me love reading, or, as it was despairingly called at the time, "escapist reading."

But how to find an outlet for all the things, spoken and unspoken, bubbling up inside me?

That was the question.

Go back and re-read the quotation from Hawthorne that begins this essay and you'll see how the rest of this whole essay really is just commentary.

Chapter 7
"Steve-o"

Nobody I know calls him "Steve-o." I never called him "Steve-o." To me, he was and always will be "Steve King."

After stumbling through all the usual nightmares, real and imagined, in junior high and high school, I ended up at the University of Maine in Orono. Throughout high school— ever since I was a little kid, actually—I had always drawn and painted pictures. Sure, all kids do that, but I (and others around me, particularly my mother) saw and encouraged me in art. I suppose I had a modicum of talent, and I certainly had the drive to create because of all the things, dark and light, roiling in my imagination.

I was looking for an outlet, and drawing seemed to be it.

Rockport, Massachusetts, in case you didn't know, is (or at least was) known as an artist's colony. If you've ever been to Bearskin Neck, you've seen the galleries, but when I was growing up in the Fifties and Sixties, there were plenty of active painters in town, and you could go to the Rockport Art Association and see their work on display. When I was ten or eleven, I even posed to have my portrait painted by students in an art class. Probably got paid fifty cents for sitting there for a couple of hours. It was hell, I remember that much.

Drawing and art seemed to be the thing. I had been (and still am, to this day) impressed—nay, blown away by the art-work I first encountered on the covers of the Ace Burroughs books. Frank Frazetta and Roy Krenkel were *great* "illustrators."

(Side note: I make a clear distinction between "illustrators" and "artists" the same way I make a distinction between "authors" and "writers." I side solidly with "writers" and "illustrators"—the blue collar working people in the arts.)

All through high school, I had my sights set on being a commercial artist. The daughter of someone my mother knew painted pictures for Hallmark Greeting Cards. I thought even that would be a much better job than…I don't know…being "backsight" man on a surveying team.

So in my senior year, I applied to all the art schools I could. Mass Art…RISDI…At the same time my biology teacher (Frank Morgan) said he was impressed with my work in his Advanced Biology class. (I think it was because I could draw some really cool pictures of what I was seeing through the microscope.) He was a graduate of the University of Maine, and he encouraged me to apply there to study Biology. Since the father of my girlfriend at the time (Geneva Parker) was also a graduate of U.M.O. and her brother Russ was currently a student there, I decided to apply. I also applied to the University of Massachusetts as a "safety" school.

Then the crisis of confidence (remember my bugbear of "low self-esteem") and a bureaucratic slipup sealed my fate.

I was scheduled to show my portfolio at the art schools where I had applied, and I didn't have what I thought was "admission quality" work. There were two other "artists" in my class—the previously mentioned Frank Sheldon and Alan Crane. Simply put—these guys were *way* better than I was. I couldn't compete, and thinking—knowing that I would be up against people even better than Frank and Alan, I chickened out. I blew off my portfolio interviews. Just didn't show up.

When I hadn't heard from my safety school, UMass, I contacted the admissions office and was informed that they never got my application. So the autumn after my high school graduation in 1966, by default, I was off to the University of Maine in Orono...the only college into which I had been accepted.

It felt like I'd been given a four-year sentence to a gulag in Siberia. Remember, this was long before cell phones, personal computers and the Internet, Facebook and Twitter. While all my high school friends went off to Clark (where my middle son Jesse eventually went—great school!), Dartmouth, Harvard, UConn, Springfield College, and even my safety school, UMass, I was off to the Great Tundra in northern Maine. Wow!

Freshman year was hell. I hated Maine and just about everyone there. I was not a good student. Remember? I wasn't even half the student my sister and brother were. I was mentally and socially insecure, immature, out of my depth, lonely, sad, depressed and yeah—horny. I still liked girls, and believe me, I saw girls on campus I still dream about. (Good thing I haven't seen them recently; the reality would destroy the illusion).

It wasn't homesickness in the classic sense. I had gone away to summer camp since I was eight years old, so I was used to being away from home and my parents. Besides, I didn't have to help my dad surveying...except on those weekends I came home to visit. I just hated Maine because I was so far away from... everything. As rustic and bucolic as my childhood had been, I grew up about an hour out of Boston. We went to Red Sox and Bruins games when I was a kid—I even saw Ted Williams and Mickey Mantle play! So Maine was...way out of it!

I had a room—number 311—in Gannett Hall. Also in that same dorm was a guy you simply couldn't help but notice. He was tall and lanky, had greasy black hair, and a hunched-over posture that seemed like an attempt to hide his true height—which was impressively tall. I first noticed the guy in the line for meals at the "Commons." What was unusual—or at least note-worthy from my point of view was that every day, every meal, he would stand in line with his nose buried in a paperback book.

Yeah!

And they were the kinds of books *I* read!

I found out this guy's name was Steve King, and even though I suspected he was a kindred spirit I didn't "make friends" with him. (I was—and remain—rather socially awkward. You know, a Finnish extrovert is the guy who will look at *your* shoes when he talks to you). But Steve and I were (surprise!) both English majors. I didn't start out as an English major. I enrolled in the College of Life Sciences and Agriculture to study Biology (Easy acceptance). During my sophomore year, when I was struggling academically and trying to stay in school to keep my student deferment so my sorry ass didn't end up in Vietnam, I took a literature class with Professor Judy Hakola. (A Finn name, but she was married to a Finn, so that was good enough for me!) Judy encouraged me, told me I had a knack for writing, said I was a perceptive reader, and maybe I should consider major-ing in English. Since I was at the point of flunking out and being "invited" to travel to sunny Southeast Asia, I thought that might be a good idea. When I saw Judy again a while back, we had a good laugh over my reaction to her suggestion.

I said: "You mean I can get a degree just…*reading?*"

Okay, I wasn't the brightest bulb but I was amazed at the concept of being an English major because from junior high school on (with the exception of Fred Ives), none of my English teachers encouraged me to read all that "crazy S.F. stuff." They wanted me to read "lit-ra-chure."

Suddenly, the prospect of reading and writing—two things I always "just did"—was inviting, so I switched majors. And I did all right, grades-wise. And I noticed this Steve King guy was making himself known on campus. His contributions to the student "literary" magazine (famously titled "Onan") always stood out as exceptional. And when we had anti-war rallies, it seemed like Steve was often the first to grab the microphone and start ranting away against the war. I envied him his "extroversion."

Look, Steve had raw writing talent even then, and he was gregarious, and he hung out with the "cool" people on campus—the people who snubbed me and who wouldn't accept me. I didn't really know that. I assumed they were too cool for me. I may have been cool, too, but I doubt it. I was just a fear-filled goober who read S.F. During the summer of my sophomore year, I started surfing, so—yeah, I got cool at least for a while, but that was more by association.

Back to Steve. We weren't close friends. We never had classes together. We didn't hang out together. We didn't party or "trip" together. But I knew who he was, and I guess he knew who I was, and when I was in grad school studying for my Master's in English, Steve did something that totally changed my life.

Chapter 8
"What Steve Did"

I don't want this essay to be about Steve King, but when I was in graduate school, he sold Carrie to Doubleday. Come on, you King freaks—What year was it? 1973? 1974? Somewhere around then.

I knew before then that Steve had been selling stories to some of the raunchy skin mags, and I read his work in the student literary magazine. His stuff was amazing and seemed to be printed in a different typeface or different color ink because even back then—and *not* with the benefit of hindsight—I knew way back then that his work stood out from all the rest. The one time I submitted something to the student lit mag, I missed the deadline, so it was rejected. I didn't believe the editor. I figured they hated my writing, and if I couldn't place my writing in the goddamned student magazine, I was a complete loser as a writer.

But when Steve sold a *real* novel...to a *real* New York publisher and was edited by a *real* New York editor...Damn! That was a revelation that went sort of like this: "Holy shit! You don't have to be a Dead White Guy to be published. You can be a geeky kid from the University of Maine (yes, Steve was geeky too) and if what you write is good enough, then—goddamn, a New York publisher might actually *pay* you for it!"

For the first time in my life, I decided to try to write something and sell it.

It was a real possibility...but it wasn't that easy.

As Yoda says, "Do...or do not. There is no try."

Chapter 9
"Where I Went Wrong"

All writers, when they're starting out, make mistakes, but the first mistake is saying (because that means you're thinking it) that you are "trying" to write or that you "want to" write.

We all know the first rule of writing: Writers write.

Applying the seat of your pants to a chair is essential. Having something to write on (a computer, a pad of paper, birch bark) is also a necessity. But it's the ideas…oh, the ideas.

Any published author, when interviewed, gets asked the inevitable, unanswerable question: "Where do you get your ideas?

I know about that Post Office box in Schenectady, New York, but I have a few pat answers:

Inside my head.

I stop going to the bathroom for a few days and everything just backs up.

They just come to me.

I get them from my dreams.

I'll leave it to you to decide which if (any) of these are true, at least for me, but I do know where I got the idea for my first novel, *Moondeath*. (Yes! I hate that title and several of the other titles my editor(s) at Zebra/Kensington foisted on me. *Moonwalker*?...Cracker, please!). But before I get to relating how the first novel came about, I should probably tell you a little about the writing I did before I sold anything. It's instructive (I think).

Starting in grad school (and I don't need to research this

one: I know I was there from 1971 to 1974), I dabbled with writing. I mean—come on. I was an English grad student. If I didn't at least *aspire* to write, what good was I? I remember two ideas for novels I had that, I think, might have been good if I had ever worked them out.

The first idea was a science fiction/adventure about a world that had been devastated by nuclear war. The only survivors were the Inuit...Eskimos, and I posited a world where Eskimo culture expanded and took over the world. I don't know if the term "global climate change" had been coined yet, but we may have had "nuclear winter." In any event, I had three astronauts who were in space, and (like in *Planet of the Apes*) returned to find their civilization gone—blasted away—and they had to adapt to the new culture.

Not bad, and prescient maybe, but the other idea I got—and this was in 1974, mind you—involved a man who had lost vital brain functions in an accident. He had portions of his brain replaced with "radio devices" that, I envisioned, would communicate with a huge computer that would allow him to function.

Now here's the kicker.

The computer, it turned out, was connected to other computers by telephone lines, thus creating a whole system of interconnected computers. In my story, the computer system had become self-aware, and realizing it now controlled a person, it had a "body" it could use as an assassination tool or whatever to protect its ever-expanding intelligence.

Even now, I don't think those are bad ideas, but I certainly wasn't at a point with my creativity where I could sit down and *write* them.

I also dabbled with short stories, but, truth to tell, they were astonishingly stupid. I sent them out and garnered my share of (deserved) rejections from *Analog, F&SF,* and *The New Yorker.* Yeah …I actually sent some poems (all bad) to *The New Yorker.* Want to read one?

But it was somewhere around this time that I heard about Steve selling *Carrie* and I began in earnest to "think" about writing. When Steve's second novel, *'Salem's Lot,* came out, I had a revelation. I got a very simple idea. If Steve had cornered the "vampires in Maine" market, then why couldn't I try my hand at "werewolves in New Hampshire?" I even joked about doing a "mummies in Vermont" novel to complete the classic monsters trilogy.

But there it was…something simple…something I could wrap my head around instead of trying to slip faulty science in a story past Ben Bova (who was editing *Analog* at the time and sent me the nicest "put me in my place" rejection letter I ever received).

Werewolves in New Hampshire.

Easy enough. For two summers while I was college, I worked at Camp Calumet, a summer camp in New Hampshire, so I knew or at least had a sense of the New Hampshire woods. Since I had taken enough college courses to be a high school English teacher (What else are you going to do with an English degree if you don't write?), I thought I'd make my protagonist a teacher.

Write what you know. That's what they say.

Now I haven't mentioned that I had gotten married between my years as an undergrad and graduate student. I could joke and refer to my ex-wife as "She-Who-Must-Not-Be Named," but that wouldn't be nice. Although I lived to regret getting married at such a young age (I was twenty-two, for God's sake!), I got three wonderful sons—Aaron, Jesse and Matti—from the relationship, so I guess it all balances out in the end.

As it turned out, I didn't get a teaching job, but there I was married and wanting more and more to write—especially because Steve King was doing fairly well (Me—master of understatement). Keep in mind though, back then, although Steve was doing well, he wasn't "Stephen-Fucking-King" yet. I was working at the local bookstore, Waldenbooks. By "local," I mean in South Portland, Maine, where we had moved after an unsuccessful year living and studying in Cambridge, Mass. My ex-wife was a student at Harvard Divinity. I'd heard Steve and Tabby and the kids were living in Colorado, but then one day while I was at the front desk of the bookstore, in walked Steve. We started talking, catching up, and of course I told him about the novel I was working on. He—very generously—offered to read it when it was done.

Encouraged—hell yeah! I was ecstatic! Eventually the book was finished and he read it. And he liked it well enough to send it around to some editors he knew with a cover letter on his letterhead! Can't beat that! When those editors passed, after a few more years, Steve turned it over to his agent at the time, Kirby McCauley.

And *Moondeath* sold.

God, I *hate* that title, but I guess it's better than the one I came up with—*The Dark Brother*. My editor rejected it because, she said, it sounded "racist."

It took me two years to write the damned book, and then four years before I—well, Kirby—sold it—and this was with Steve's generous help and encouragement and personal pitch letter.

Let me say it here and now. I probably would not have finished, much less sold, that first book if it hadn't been for Steve's kind generosity and help. If you like my work, thank Steve for giving me a hand up when I was starting out and needed it. If you think my work sucks—it's all Steve's fault! He should have buried that damned book in his backyard.

Moondeath was a January, 1980, release, so it hit the stands in December of 1979, but here's another little piece of serendipity.

I was working at the local Waldenbooks, like I said, and well—I had a novel published. Our regional manager (whose name I am ashamed to admit I've forgotten) said it was okay if I placed the book on the front checkout desk. Back then, tracking sales and ordering in bookstores was not done by computer, but any regional sales spike showed up on the company reports. Because I was pushing the hell out of *Moondeath* in our one little store in Maine, *Moondeath* became a required title for the entire chain of Waldenbooks.

Zebra, who was pretty much just starting out back then with their horror novels, was caught by surprise. They actually had to GO BACK FOR A SECOND PRINTING to fill all those orders for Waldenbooks. Although I didn't make the *Times* list, and the advance I got was pathetic...especially since all I had to compare it to what Steve was getting per book. Remember, *Carrie* sold to NAL paperback for $400,000. Sure, half of that went to Doubleday, but still, that was a righteous chunk of change. I got $2,500.00 up front for *Moondeath* and a sweet 8%/10% royalty split. (that means I got 8% of the cover price for sales up to 100,000 copies and 10% of the cover price over 100K. Try getting *that* today for a paperback original.) The book earned out and earned a decent, but not great, royalty. It got reviewed, I got interviewed locally. People started calling me "Maine's other horror writer." I even got a movie nibble or two. Still, I had to keep my day job. I was frustrated that I couldn't write full-time because, by now, my brain was teeming with ideas, many of which entered a notebook I kept (and still keep) and became full novels many years later.

So *Moondeath* did what it did. I wished/hoped it had made more money, and I was frustrated/upset that it didn't. But it did well enough that Zebra wanted another book from me, and a year or two later...(God, talk about horrible titles!)...*Moonbog* was published. Imagine using that title in England.

Sophomore novel. Lofty ambitions. Faulty execution.

'Nuff said.

But *Moonbog* (my original title was *The Bog Man*—ugh to that, too!) sold, and it sold well enough that it looked like I'd be writing paperback originals for small amounts of money and never sell a thing to the movies and somehow manage to scrape together a living by staying at the bookstore. Of course, by now, my first son had been born, so I had a few additional pressures to write and be a real success...or else keep my "real job" to support my family.

I think, in the end, I did the right thing by finding a balance between those two positions.

Chapter 10
"A New Dimension in Promotion"

Then it looked like, after two books, I was finally going to make it. This is where the tale takes a few sad twists and turns, oh my brothers and sisters…Sad because, given a different psychological makeup, I might have been able to make things work out better than they did.

Instead, I lost.

I was on the merry-go-round, and when I had a chance to grab the brass ring…I missed it.

It started with some agent shenanigans. You see, I knew (was convinced, anyway) that Kirby, Steve's agent, had taken on my first two books only as a favor to Steve, not out of any genuine interest in my writing or me. (Damn, there's that low self-esteem creeping in here like a stray cat. I thought I chased it out of the house.) So after *Moonbog* sold, Kirby cut what he said were his "unproductive" clients. He farmed us out to different agencies, and I ended up with Martha Millard.

At the time, I was working on the book that would eventually become *Nightstone*. My working title was *The Menhir*, but my editor nixed that idea, and probably rightfully so. Another working title was *The Dreaming Stone*. In any event, I was agitating to get a better advance. Don't kid yourselves. If a publisher gives you a crap advance, it means that your promotion and advertising will be crap (or nil). When I finished *Nightstone*, I sent the finished draft to Martha, and she had a soul-crushing response to the book. I still have the letter, and could quote it directly if I felt inclined to dig it out, but what she said in essence was that the book was *not* my breakout book and—here comes the crusher—SHE WASN'T SURE I HAD A BREAK-OUT BOOK IN ME.

Try swallowing that when you already have self-esteem issues and are feeling as though you wouldn't be published except as a favor to Steve King.

Needless to say, Martha and I parted company. I learned one valuable lesson. I wrote a two or three page letter, ranting and raving at Martha, calling her every bad name I could think of, and telling her she didn't know shit from shoe polish, and that she was the worst agent in the world, and that she should—not eat shit and die, but eat shit and *live*.

Then I tore up the letter and sent her a one-sentence response, which I can quote exactly.

"I accept your resignation as my literary agent."

Simple, clean, and—at least in public—no hard feelings. A few years later, I met Martha at a science fiction convention… back when I went to conventions; I don't anymore except for NECon. At that con, I introduced Martha to a friend as "my ex-wife." She was not amused, and we haven't spoken since.

But I did have faith in my writing…or I was at least desperate enough to have to keep writing because I couldn't get hired to teach full-time, and I was stagnating in the bookstore. So I reworked *Nightstone* and found a new agent—Dominick Abel. We tried to sell *Nightstone* to someone other than Zebra, but got no offers, so we went back to Zebra and took what I thought was a pitifully small offer of $5K and the usual 8%/10% royalty split.

But then Zebra did something extraordinary.

They slapped an original hologram onto the cover and they promoted the hell out of it.

Keep in mind that they were doing this even though they had paid me a lousy advance. And truth to tell, I honestly felt as though they didn't give a rat's ass what was beneath their hologram cover. The book had an initial print run just shy of a million copies. It was everywhere. It got promoted (the cover hologram did, at least, and I was happy my novel was the one "under the cover") and it sold like a muthafucka. It went back to press several times, and it kept selling. I did a small promotional tour in New England. I was interviewed. I was...so I thought... finally going to "make it."

But here's where I made a colossal mistake.

Because of the publicity for the cover, other publishers came a'courtin'.

Yes, I was feeling as though I was finally on the verge of making it, but I was convinced that in the greater scheme of things, it didn't matter a cat's fart that *I* had written the book. All that mattered was the hologram. Low self-esteem kicked in, and I was depressed instead of elated by the success of *Night-stone*. So when Warner Books threw an offer at me that made my head spin ($75,000 for two books with the usual 8%/10% split), I went for it.

The first danger looming on the horizon was that prior to the success of *Nightstone*, I had signed a contract for two more books with Zebra. I was already well into—if not fin-ished with—the first of these two books, *Little Brothers* (My original title, and I still like it). So I would owe Zebra one more book after *Little Brothers* before I could write my two books for Warner.

Here's where I made my big mistake: I was honest.

I knew word of the Warner deal would eventually leak out, so I confessed to my editor that after the book that followed *Little Brothers*, I'd be leaving Zebra.

Now stoked with the success of the hologram and sales of *Nightstone*, Zebra was all set to put a FULL-COVER hologram on *Little Brothers*. They even sent me the cover flat. Once they knew I was leaving, though, the (making the wise business decision) decided to give the full cover hologram to someone else. Ruby Jean Jensen, as I recall.

Good for her.

(Editor's note: The full-cover hologram was used on Ruby Jean Jensen's *House of Illusions*.)

And why would Zebra promote an author who was leaving them?

Why spend a single cent on me?

I wouldn't be surprised if, during an editorial meeting or two and around the Zebra offices, the words "Fuck Hautala!" were said and agreed to with great frequency. Or maybe they didn't even care. They could move on to promoting another author who was a bit more loyal or less honest. As long as they made money, who cares *who* wrote it?

When *Little Brothers* hit the stands, its initial print run was approximately 10% of what *Nightstone*'s had been. That meant that for every ten people who bought and hopefully read and enjoyed *Nightstone*, nine of them wouldn't be able to buy *Little Brothers* even if they wanted to because there weren't enough copies!

Needless to say, the sales figures plummeted. I had done what I had thought was the right thing by telling my editor at

Zebra that I had signed with Warner, and I had...and would continue to...and maybe still am paying the price for that "mistake"...if, that is, you think that being honest and up front in business is ever a mistake.

I don't...no matter the cost, and have proven it over and over again, at least to myself, if not publicly.

The follow-up novel—and I thought the last book I would do for Zebra—to *Little Brothers* was *Moonwalker*. Back to the goddamned "Moon" titles. My working titles were *Night Siege* (hoping to trade on the "Night" title) or simply, *The Siege*. I don't think Zebra was trying to trade on my past book titles with a "Moon" title. I think they came up with it because the same month *Moonwalker* came out, a Michael Jackson (God rest) biography also came out.

Honest I may be, but I am cynical enough to be convinced to this day that my editor at Zebra forced the title of *Moonwalker* on me simply because she was hoping people would order and buy my horror novel, thinking they were getting the Michael Jackson biography.

In the end, *Moonwalker* sold even fewer copies than *Little Brothers*, so by the time *Winter Wake*, my first novel for Warner (and my choice of title again!) came out, the Warner sales force couldn't give the book away (not that they printed galleys or did much promotion, anyway). I owed Warner two books, so after the disastrous sales for *Winter Wake*, I wrote *Dead Voices* already knowing that Warner didn't want to continue to work with me and that sales would tank even further.

The axe was poised above my head, and it was about to fall several times just to make sure my spinal cord was severed.

Chapter 11
"I Find a Home"

Fuck, that last section was depressing. Let's shift gears…Let's open the windows and let in a little air. Let's mix our metaphors, too, shall we?

Around the time I wrote (and published) *Moondeath*, I started attending science fiction conventions. I figured I had to network and socialize and meet people whose work I had read and admired, and meet some people whose work I thought sucked (and still do). Yeah, I can be catty. So sue me.

I met a few writers who also lived in Maine—mostly "sky-fi," as Tom Monteleone calls it. There was Tom Easton, who reviewed books for my old standby *Analog*. (I still buy and at least skim *Analog* today, but it's not like the "good old days" for me.) There was Barry B. Longyear, who I am glad to see is starting to publish again. And there was William R. "Bill" Fortschen, who started out publishing a trilogy for Del Rey Books and now writes NYT bestsellers with Newt Gingrich. Bill always joked about being "to the far right of Genghis Khan." I guess he proved it. But politics aside, Bill and I became friends, and we started going to Boskone, an annual SF convention in Boston.

There were years when I could afford a hotel room. There was one year when I stayed at a friend's apartment in Cambridge. And then there was the year I slept in the all-night movie theatre because I couldn't afford a hotel room. I think that was the year the World Science Fiction Convention was in Boston. That was also the year my agent, Kirby McCauley, invited me to a private party for his clients and guests. It's also where I first met someone who today (in spite of *his* politics) is closer to me than my own brother—Tom Monteleone.

Ever the low self-esteem guy, I stumbled around Kirby's party in a daze. There were authors there that I read and admired—Joe Halderman, for one. George Takei was there. And there was Tom. This was back in the pre-Elizabethan era, so I can't tell you anything about the numerous adventures I've had with Tom, including that trip to a little...let's say "venue" in Hawthorne, California. And I didn't really get to know Tom until he approached me at my first NECon. That's a story in and of itself. I've told it too many times, but will give it to you one more time...for the last time!

But back to Boskone for a moment.

I think it was in 1981—it might have been later, at one of the "pro" parties (You know—those "invite only" parties publishers, editors, and agents throw for , I guess, the tax write-off...the parties where one writer said to me, "They spend our royalties.") I met Ginjer Buchanan. She, and later that same weekend, Craig Shaw Gardner, told me about this little "horror" convention called NECon. They both urged me to attend, and—thankfully—I registered. Again, I forget the exact year, but a little research will turn it up. I'll get to NECon in a moment, but first, I want to tell you about another "brother from a different mother" I met.

It was through Ginjer.

At some Boskone or other, she mentioned that she was publishing a horror novel and asked if I read it and liked it, would I be willing to offer a blurb. I was flattered. It's always nice to be asked for a blurb. That means *someone* thinks your name on their book will help sell copies. That's the theory, anyway, and this was my first time "blurbing."

I had been asked to blurb one book before this. I forget the author, but whatever book it was, I read it and liked it at least enough to send a blurb to the editor. Problem is, that blurb "got lost" or "never arrived." Once I found this out, I was determined not to let that happen again, so I asked Ginjer for the author's address so I could CC him on the blurb.

That author was some guy named Matthew J. Costello, and the book was *Beneath Still Waters*.

I read it and liked it and blurbed it, but I sent the blurb to both Ginjer and Matt just to be safe. I also included a letter to Matt because I recognized his name. He was the game reviewer for *Analog*.

Yes! My *Analog*!

I realized that I was brushing elbows with SOMEONE FAMOUS…someone who had actually been published in *Analog*!

As it turns out, Matt and I struck up a correspondence and later a phone relationship, and eventually we started hanging out…at conventions, at each other's house, whatever. And—like Tom—I knew I'd met a brother. Through the years, I've met a lot of other folks because of my writing. I won't begin to name names because I will inevitably leave someone out, and I don't want this to be a Who's Who list. Suffice to say that Matt and Tom are my two oldest and dearest friends—in or out of the business.

But brothers and sisters need a home, and this "little convention" Ginjer and Craig told me about turned out to be that home.

Of course, when I first started coming to NECon, I felt a bit out of it. You see, I labored under this impression that I honestly believe to this day.

I don't think...No, strike that. I *know* I would not have been published when I was—or maybe ever—if it hadn't been for Steve King. So when I went to NECon, I felt like an intruder, an imposter, a fraud, a loser, a turd in the punchbowl...all those wonderful thoughts and emotions that still swirl just below the surface.

Why I feel that way is between me and my shrink. I have a handle on it and I'm coping. Like I said at the start of this, you would *think* being a Finn was terrifying enough.

Now this first NECon. It must have been in 1985 because I had the hologram from *Nightstone* on my nametag.

A little side note: I don't wear a nametag at NECon for two...make that three reasons:

Nametags are uncomfortable as all hell, always flapping around on your chest like a bat, clinging to your shirt...and that elastic string clinging to your neck like a miniature noose bugs me.

One year at Boskone, when Craig Gardner and I were asked who we were when we were trying to get into a publishers party, Craig responded by saying "Badges? We don't need no steenkin' *badges*! I thought that was hilarious and I took the sentiment to heart because it was a funny "Do *you* know who we *are*?" moment. And —

I figure, especially at NECon, if anyone doesn't know who I am by now, I probably don't want to meet them and they probably don't want to meet me. I have enough trouble catching up with old friends at NECon, and I am uncomfortable going around introducing myself and "getting to know" people. Maybe it's a "the mountain will come to Muhammad" thing. I don't know.

Granted, there's a heavy dose of egotism in Reasons #2 and 3, but low self-esteem often hides a raging ego problem. (I am nothing if not filled with contradictions.)

Anyway, so there I was at my first NECon and I was having my fair share of awkward moments when this guy Tom Monteleone staggered up to me. Now I remembered Tom from Kirby's party, but he obviously didn't remember me. That fit right into my low self-esteem, *no-one-cares-who-I-am* mode. That night, Tom was feeling no pain as he drifted over to me and clapped his arm around my shoulders. Pointing to the hologram on my nametag, he said, "I know that fuckin' book! I read that fuckin' book! It's a great fuckin' book!" (Or words to that effect.)

His breath was more like diesel fumes than alcohol. Yes. He'd been hitting the Dickel harder than he'd been hitting on any women…at least at that point in the festivities (Oops…that was pre-Elizabethan.).

Anyway, I muttered my thanks, embarrassed because… well, I'm Finnish, and Tom, being Sicilian, was a little more demonstrative than I was (or am). I wanted to believe he genuinely liked the book, but in my heart of hearts, I doubted he'd even read it and was bullshitting me. I assume anyone who tells me they like any of my books must be bullshitting me.

But that wasn't the end of it. Tom leaned closer, our noses almost touching, and said: "You gotta have a fuckin' drink with me," and raised a bottle of Dickel.

I had my usual beer (I prefer microbrews) and muttered my thanks again and said something about how I was all set with a beer. (Damn! As I'm writing this in August, 2009, it is *the* hottest day of the summer so far, and now all I can think about is a tall, frosty, cold one.)

"But you gotta have a fuckin' Dickel with me," Tom said.

Once again, I told him thanks, but no thanks, that I was all set, and added that I never drank distilled alcohol. I only drank beer. (This was years before Holly and I went to St. Kitts and I discovered the true wonders of dark rum.)

"No, no, no!" Tom pressed uncomfortably close...for a Finn at least. "You *gotta* have a drink of Dickel with me!"

He obviously wasn't taking *no* for an answer, but I kept insisting that I was fine with my beer, nice to meet you, thanks for liking my book (even if you didn't really read it).

So Tom clamped my neck firmly with one hand and pulled my face even closer to his and said: "Lemme ask you somethin'. Have you ever run your hand up the inner thigh of an eighteen-year-old girl?"

Now I have got to tell you, the Finn in me was freaking the fuck out because of the physical closeness. (I already told you about the extrovert Finn who will look at *your* shoes when he talks to you.) Now this suddenly very personal question threw me for a loop.

But when Tom said, "Well? Have you?" I had to answer.

Blushing, I'm sure, I stumbled and stammered and eventually said something like "Well, yeah...sure."

After belching another blast of alcohol fumes into my face, Tom leaned back, smiled and said: "Well, then... I guess I don't have to tell you how smooth this drink is."

That was the first—and definitely not the last—time I drank a shot of Dickel with Tom Monteleone, and that was when I first realized: *Hey! This NECon might not be such a bad place to hang out after all.*

Since then I've attended all but one NECon. There are too many funny stories to relate…too many friends I've met…and too many we've lost along the way (Charlie, I miss you!) for me to go into great detail.

Leave it at this: NECon is the only place in the world where for four days out of the year, I feel absolutely accepted for who and what I am, even by people who don't read my books or who have read them and don't like them.

It's my true family.

Chapter 12
"The Texians"

I wasn't just writing (or, as they say, "trying" to write) and going to conventions, trying to feel like I fit in somewhere. I also was still married, had kids (final tally—that I know of—is three), and wasn't making enough to live on exclusively by writing, so I had to work.

My workaholic father formed my attitudes toward work. Coming out of the Great Depression (he graduated high school in 1929—what luck!), he imbued me with all sorts of notions, the strongest of which is YOU NEVER STOP WORKING. He worked tirelessly, eighty-hour weeks, and he expected—or made me feel as though he expected—me to do the same.

That was easy when I was in college. The war in Southeast Asia was crackling along, and I had a student deferment, and the last thing I wanted to do was lose that and end up drafted and sent to Vietnam. I had friends who that happened to. They didn't come back the same. Some of them were better people, having seen the world, met interesting people, and killed them. Most of them came back changed in profound and not so good ways. One friend of mine from high school put a gun to his head and pulled the trigger because he couldn't live with what he saw—and did—in 'Nam.

But in order to stay in school and keep that valued deferment—at least until the draft lottery was installed…luckily, that was one lottery I *didn't* win—I had to work hard. I also had to work hard because I wasn't half the student my sister and brother were. If this whole right brain/left brain thing is for real, I no doubt have a "double right" brain. I have so little left brain for logical functions that I can barely balance a checkbook after I've written only two or three checks.

I had to work hard. It's always taken me two or three times as long to read and absorb…anything. Even with writing, it takes me twice as long to come up with something that's only third rate.

AUTHOR'S NOTE: I will continually display my keenly developed low self-esteem. If it's bugging you—sorry. Go read something else.

So besides writing, I had day jobs, all of which made me miserable, mostly because I wanted to be home writing. I worked at various bookstores (Waldenbooks, Booksmith, and Borders), I taught: one year full-time junior high English, many years as an adjunct faculty in English at the University of Southern Maine, Southern Maine Community College, York County Community College, and far too many years as a substitute teacher in junior and senior high schools in Westbrook, Gorham and Falmouth.

I also had real crap jobs, like bank messenger, bakery manager for a grocery store (that lasted about six months), mason's tender (flashback to my childhood), house painter, carpenter's helper (banged my thumb silly), copy editor for a local press, dishwasher at a restaurant…all sorts of wonderful jobs that built my character.

Yeah.

All I wanted to do was write, and then—when *Nightstone* sold, like over a million copies, I was ready to write full-time forever. That didn't last long because of bad choices my ex-wife and especially I made at the time. And when things fell apart writing-wise (sales in the tank—contracts for not nearly as much as I needed to survive), things fell apart relationship-wise too.

I lost my house, my marriage dissolved...the only thing that kept me hanging on in those bleakest times were...well a few things. In no particular order...

My drive to write. I wasn't going to give up no matter what because writing was the only thing I could do half-well. The rest, I totally fucked up.

My kids. I have three of the best children on the planet. They're all adults now, and they make me proud daily, but they were great kids!—funny, aggravating, challenging, and just plain cool.

My friends. Here's a little piece of advice for you: When things are going great—when you're "making it"...you'll find you have a lot of friends. But when things turn (as they *always* will), you'll find out who your real friends are. I have said for many years now that, when I was at my lowest point, when I felt like Davy Crockett swinging Ole Betsy on the ramparts of the Alamo, I took a look around. I noticed who was there with me. I will list their names because I want to acknowledge their tireless friendship even when I was at my most tiresome.

Again, in no particular order: Matt Costello, Tom Monteleone, Chris Fahy, Mike Kimball, Rich Chizmar, Ed Gorman, Joe Lansdale, Bill Relling (God rest), Charlie Grant (God rest), Ginjer Buchanan, Steve Bissette, Glenn Chadbourne, Roman Ranieri, and Chris Golden. Holly and Mark and a few others came along too recently to have been at the Alamo, but they sure as hell were at the Battle of San Jacinto. (If you don't get any of the historical references, then do a little reading in history, dummy.)

To be sure, there were other friends on the ramparts as gunpowder smoke rolled in over the walls, but this was the handful of people I could see standing shoulder to shoulder with me on the walls. They were the ones I could call, and they would actually take my calls. They answered my letters. They let me stop by for a visit if I was in the neighborhood. They didn't desert me when my star was waning (Actually, my star went supernova, leaving my career a black hole…Read some science too!) These were the ones I saw there—My true friends, the Texians! I find it ironic in the extreme that two of my three sons now live in Texas.

Yes—there were other friends…mostly (but not all) people from NECon—Pete Crowther, F. Paul Wilson, Doug Winter, Steve Spruill, Gahan Wilson, the Booths, John McIlveen, Beth Massie, and so many others, but they weren't the ones who ended up with bleeding ears after listening to me moan and cry and freak out with rage.

Doesn't every writer need friends like that? This is one fucked-up, crazy-ass business with a lot more pain and frustration than satisfaction (except for the lucky few…and I wonder about them, as well!).

Honestly, if had a "real" job, a career I could "fall back on," there have been so many times I would have quit and walked away.

But I didn't.

I couldn't

Writing was all I had…especially after I lost a house and a marriage. Did I mention that my ex-wife worked for a law firm? That she got free legal advice regarding the divorce? Then I may not have mentioned that when I left the marriage—yes, I was the one who pulled the plug—I left with pretty much what I could fit into a friend's truck. Dave Hinchberger gave me a coffee cup that had a great saying. I think my ex has the cup now. It read: I STARTED OUT WITH NOTHING AND STILL HAVE MOST OF IT LEFT. So true...

God, this is getting depressing. Let me take a short break and see if when I come back I have anything nice to say.

Chapter 13
"Bambi's Mother's Advice"

My mother took my sister, my brother and me to see Disney's *Bambi* when we were little. No, it wasn't the first run. I'm not that old, but I won't even pretend to remember how old I was. I must have been under five because I remember having a "Bambi" juice glass when we lived in Rockport. Of course anyone who has seen *Bambi* remembers the scene where Bambi's mother tells him to "Run…run and don't look back," and then, after a dramatic pause, we hear a single gunshot and, although we know what it means immediately, Bambi doesn't. Realization dawns… eventually.

My mother died in an accidental fall when she was in her late eighties. She was dragging a basket full of squash down into the cellar, moving down the stairs backwards a step at a time. That's how she always did it. When I was home, I would of course help her, but only my father was home that day. We figure she must have miscalculated and thought she was on the cellar floor, when, in fact, she had one more step to go. She fell over backwards and hit the back of her head on the cement cellar floor so hard it dislodged her brain stem from her brain.

But she didn't die right away.

Her heart kept beating even after she was airlifted to Brigham and Women's Hospital in Boston. The family gathered to be at her bedside, but—of course—she never regained consciousness. We met with the doctors, who told us they could keep her alive indefinitely, but there was no hope. The nerves in her spinal column were basically disconnected from her brain.

She was gone.

So the family authorized her to be taken off life support. The nurse said her heart would only continue to beat for fifteen or twenty minutes.

It kept beating for over an hour. The nurse whispered to me that I'd better hope I inherited her cardiovascular system. I do hope that, but my mother's "heart"—both literally and symbolically—is my strongest memory of her. If my father was the brains and brawn of the family, she was the heart and emotion. She was the one who taught me to value my dreams and what they tell me.

I was devastated by my mother's death.

No one realized it at the time, but I quit writing for a full year. By this point in my career, I didn't think I had the heart to write any more. I'd done what I could do; I'd had my high point (Selling over a million copies of *Nightstone* was no mean feat); and I'd had the bottom drop out of my career and my life. My mother was the center of our family, and without her I felt cast adrift.

So I stopped writing.

And nobody missed me or my writing.

Except for "The Texians." Those friends were there for me, calling and writing and asking me how I was doing.

I was doing a lot worse than any of them probably knew. My career tanking was one thing, but losing my mother was too much. I started seeing a therapist (which didn't seem to help) and taking antidepressants (which definitely didn't help). I was suicidal, but instead I got a full-time job at Borders Books and vowed never to write again. There was no point.

Here's the biggest lesson I learned from that time.

I'm not all that important.

No one is all that important.

Except for the handful of family and friends whose hearts and lives are connected.

My marriage was underwater at this point. But my sons and my father and my sister and (to a degree) my brother all helped me pull my head out of my ass. I don't mean to disparage grief, but I'm the kid who cried when Lassie came home.

I took (and still take) everything to heart. Besides not being half the student my sister and brother were, I was also told—by everyone during my childhood—that I was "too sensitive."

And it's true. Sure, I laugh and joke, and words said in jest are easily sloughed off, even if they are cuttingly true, but words said in anger or frustration cut me a lot deeper than a) they should, and b) is probably healthy.

So I was in the depths of grief, and I was working at Borders, and I was absofuckinglutely miserable.

And then two of The Texians got in touch with me.

Chicken or egg, I don't know which came first, but in my mind these were the two lifelines that people threw to me. They not only helped me get out of my depression; they were also the two events that, for better or worse (and I know there are some "critics" who will say for worse) got me writing again.

One Texian was Rich Chizmar, at Cemetery Dance Publications.

You see, back in the *Winter Wake/Dead Voices* times, when I first learned that Warner didn't want any more books from me because *Winter Wake* (one of my personal favorites) sold "disappointingly," I got the idea to write a novel under a pseudonym to try to change tracks...or get back on the track, really (if you'll excuse me mangling the metaphor). I had written a short novel titled *The Mountain King*. I even got an offer for it, but turned it down because I thought it wasn't enough money.

(Boy, did I have more lessons in that regard coming my way!)

But Rich called, out of the blue, and asked if I had a "trunk novel" he could do as a limited for CD.

Did I?

You bet, so I sent him the manuscript for *The Mountain King*. Steve Bissette (another Texian, remember) did some great artwork, and the book came out. Eventually Leisure did a paperback edition, but apparently my low sales figures held strong. But doing that book for CD, revising it and seeing it published, got me back in the game along with a phone call from another Texian.

Ginjer Buchanan called and said she'd been talking about doing original novels based on the series *Poltergeist: The Legacy*.

I hadn't seen the show. I'm not much of a TV person. After the nightly news, it's pretty much *The Daily Show* and *The Colbert Report*, which I record the night before, and then *Countdown with Keith Olbermann*, and then finally a movie on HBO or Showtime (maybe) or (more likely) time to read.

But they sent me some tapes, and since I had already outlined a book that could easily be "modified" into a *Poltergeist* book, I said I'd do the book. I recall clearly being of two minds though: I wanted to write again, so I said "Yes," but while my mouth was saying "Yes," my brain was saying: "Who are you kidding? You can't write! You lost whatever you had. It's gone. Forget about it. Thank Ginjer and disappear."

Like I said, for better or worse, I got back to writing. I started running, and like Bambi, I didn't look back.

Chapter 14
"Back on My Wheels"

It really is mostly a blur. I'm not good on facts and figures, and the details that stick are more emotional than intellectual. If that makes sense, good, you're still with me. But what happened then is difficult for me to piece together without doing what would feel a whole lot like homework.

I have modified what someone famous once said about writing. My version goes like this:

"Being a writer is like having overdue homework every day for the rest of your life."

Not flowing, but certainly true. If you're a writer, you have to agree, and if you're an aspiring writer, get used to it!

Following my unheralded return to writing—since no one knew I had quit for a year, and sales proved not a whole lot of people noticed I was back—more Texians helped me in ways for which I can never truly and fully thank them.

One of those Texians—Chris Golden—asked me if I would be interested in co-writing some of the books in his "Body of Evidence" series. I was at the point where I felt I had gotten over myself. I no longer felt a drive to write a book that had only MY name plastered on it. I accepted that having a book sell a gazillion copies and making the *New York Times* bestseller list just wasn't going to happen.

I simply wanted to write, and working with Chris was good for me on many levels.

Sure, I got paid, and any writer who doesn't want to get paid is a fool.

I got to work with Chris, who is an amazingly inventive guy, and writing the handful of "Body of Evidence" books with him taught me things I never knew about writing.

Side note: From my point of view, anyway, writing never gets "*easy.*" I felt like an imposter…a phony who was getting away with something…a writer who would never have been published if his agent and a publisher hadn't done Steve King a favor. I didn't feel like *"Okay, maybe I can do this,"* until I finished my novel *Cold Whisper.* But every time I start a book or story, I feel like a beginner, and I would humbly suggest that *any* writer who thinks or acts like writing is easy is probably a fraud or just plain egotistically stupid.

Working with Chris helped me realize—again—the truth of that simple maxim: "A writer writes!"

So I wrote.

And then Ginjer Buchanan suggested that I try a book under a pseudonym, so I cooked up *The White Room*, which sold well enough for Berkley to contract three more books under my A.J. Matthews pseudonym. (The "A.J. Matthews" is derived from the names of my three sons—Aaron, Jesse and Matti.) Those books are *Looking Glass*, *Follow* and *Unbroken*. They're all out of print now, but see if you can find one or two on eBay or something. I think they're probably some of the best work I've ever done, and the editing Ginjer did helped make them better…but what do I know?

All through this time I was also writing short stories and, more recently, screenplays. More on the screenplays later. For now, I want to talk a bit about short stories and the writing process in general, because if this little piece is going to be of any interest to anyone, I should probably throw in a little bit of advice from my point of view.

Chapter 15
"The Writing Process"

I think I've made it clear: I don't think writing is easy—ever. I'll even go so far as to say that if writing ever does get easy for you, only one of two things can possibly be happening: either you're truly inspired and facile, or you're deluding yourself, and what you're writing is crap.

There are no other choices.

Sure…some days the words come easily; other days they're a struggle. The key is to keep writing. Every day. Inspired or not. Write!

Maybe I can help an aspiring writer or two with what follows. I certainly don't want to discourage anyone, but if I do discourage you…Good. If you can't take the demands of the job of writing, then get another job. One problem I see in the writing profession is that there are too many people with what I see as an amateur mindset. They're very good at dragging down the real professionals. (More on that later.)

So if writing is work, how do I go about it?

Truth is, I write differently today than I did when I was starting out. Writing is not like changing the oil of your car. That job's the same…every 3,000 miles. Writing a novel or story or screenplay is different every time you do it. Sure, after years of doing it you have certain techniques and habits, but you should always push—or at least try to push—yourself past easy habits.

If there's no challenge, there's no reward.

I've already touched on the vital question: "Where do you get your ideas?"

That's impossible to answer.

If you have a "cool idea" and you think up some "interesting people" this "cool idea" can happen to, then you're on your way. Never, never, *never* forget that your first (and possibly only) job is to tell an interesting story. If you don't know what "story" is— if you don't know the six basic parts of a story (plot, character, setting, theme, tone, and style, just so's you know), then forget about being a writer.

If you aren't an avid reader—of all sorts of books and stories and magazines and cereal boxes—then maybe you should forget about it.

If you don't have "something" seething inside you (you don't know what—you have to write to find out what it is) that is going to come out one way or another, and writing a story is more appealing to you than climbing to the roof of a tall building with a rifle and scope—then maybe you should forget about it.

If you think fame and fortune are just around the corner because your idea or story is "so-o-o-o fucking incredible" and now *all* you have to do is write it, then maybe you should forget about it.

If you think what your story is about—your *theme*—or how you've written the story—your *style*—is more important than putting interesting people into interesting situations, then maybe you should forget about it.

If you think that all you have to do is start the story and the character will take over and write the story for you, then maybe you should forget about it...and have some tests done to see if you're a schizophrenic.

If you don't understand the simple dictum that the best stories are a balance of both the surprising *and* the inevitable (not too much of one or the other), then maybe you should forget about it.

Once you've cut through all that (or conclude that I'm an asshole who doesn't know what the fuck he's talking about), you may be one of those unfortunates who just *has* to write.

From the beginning of my career until today, I did have one goal that I enforced whenever I could. I make myself write at least 2,000 words every time I sit down to write. Mark that I didn't say "every day." I usually do write seven days a week, but not always. Sometimes I take short vacations from writing— usually not for long—a few days, tops.

Before the advent of computers, I used to "guesstimate" my word count. Since a typical manuscript page has about 250 words, my goal was eight to ten pages a day. Now, with computers that have "word count," I start every working day and write until I get *at least* 2,000 words.

Some days—especially if I'm in the middle of a story—the words come quickly, and writing is fun.

Other days, the words come very, very slowly.

Regardless, I stay at the desk (or in the Morris chair in the living room with my laptop) until I have *at least* 2,000 words.

Never less than 2,000.

Sometimes (usually) more. I think my best day writing, I cranked out over six thousand words, but no one can keep that pace and remain sane.

Once I reach my mandatory word count for the day, I can tell myself I'm done; I've done my job, so I can relax now…keep writing if I feel like it…go with the flow or—if the day hasn't gone particularly well—quit for the day.

So that's rule number one. Two thousand words a day. No less. Usually more.

And I always try to stop writing in the middle of a chapter, scene, and sometimes even in the middle of a sentence. That way I will feel the fire in my belly and be compelled to get back to work the next day.

But a legitimate question may be: How do I know *what* to write?

Oops, I just did a word count and discovered that I've already written 2.398 words today. Since it's as hot and humid as the Amazonian Basin today (for the record, I'm writing this section on August 18, 2009), I'm heading out to the deck to smoke a cigar and do some reading. I'll pick this up tomorrow.

Okay, I'm back. Where was I?

I'll re-read the last paragraph and pick up where I left off.

That's how I do it, anyway. Don't think you have to do it this way. It's just what works for me, and if it doesn't work for you, fine. Go find your own method. The key is to keep writing. Push on to the end. Don't worry about crafting gorgeous sentences as you go. On a first draft, your goal is to plow through to the end. Worry about coming back and doing the cleanup after you have typed "The End" for the first time. (There will be several more times.)

I realize that I haven't explained very well how I get the ideas so I know where I'm going and I know what I'll write. That comes under the heading of "Outlining," which I think deserves a separate section, just so these "chapter" divisions won't be too long.

Chapter 16
"Outlines"

Let's start with a simple question.

If you live in Boston, and you have to or want to drive to L.A., would you just jump into your car and take off, fully confident that you would make it to L.A. and not end up in say, Juneau, Alaska? (I hear you can see Russia from there.)

Of course you wouldn't.

So when it comes to writing, let's keep that analogy going a little longer (and try not to mangle it). Let's consider that writing a novel is like a road trip from Boston to L.A. Sure. A short story might be the equivalent of swinging by the corner store for beer and cigarettes. But when you are tackling something as large and, frankly, intimidating as a novel, and if you want it to be good enough so someone might actually *give you money* for it—you damned well better have some kind of plan.

Now, I read several years ago what Steve King wrote in the Afterword to the first Dark Tower book. He said, in effect, that writers shouldn't outline a book. If they do, they're really just frustrated English graduate students who should be working on their thesis instead of a novel. You all have a copy of *The Gunslinger*. Look it up. I read this advice at a time when I was quite insecure about my writing.

("When is that *not* the case?" I can hear Chris Golden asking.)

But I had fewer than ten books published (the threshold when I finally stopped feeling like an imposter and accepted that I might be able to do this job), and I was still convinced that I was faking it and sooner or later would be flushed out. (I think I have been, actually, but that's for later.) What Steve wrote only magnified my near-paralyzing insecurities because—I mean... come on! This was writing advice from *Stephen King*. He sells more books in a week than I have in my entire career to date. (I may be exaggerating there; it may be that he sells more books in a day than I have so far.)

When I started my first novel—the first novel I ever finished, anyway—*Moondeath*—I used an outline. (I had two aborted novels before *Moondeath*, which I've already mentioned, neither of which I even tried to outline; I just started writing them...and then stopped after I got ten or twenty pages in because I had no fucking clue where I was going.)

Man, did I outline *Moondeath*! I remember (and still have, somewhere in the archives) the character sketches and plot outlines and maps of the town, and floor plans of every building I mentioned in the book, and timelines going back to the birth of every major character's grandparents. Lemme tell you, I outlined the *shit* out of that book!

Why?

Because I wanted to know exactly where I was going. I had every single chapter and every single scene blocked out on a separate sheet of paper in a notebook, with details as to what they were wearing, what the weather was like, the time of day, what someone was smoking or drinking. I would shuffle the pages to get the scenes in what I thought was the best order. I would reshuffle. Get new ideas. Add them. Cut out other ideas. Try to tie up loose ends. Drop stuff I no longer liked.

You get the idea. My outline was pretty much a first draft.

So then all I had to do was smooth the rough edges, blend it all together, and *presto* it was a finished first draft.

Do I outline like that now?

Of course not.

But I still will never start a book until I know where it's going.

Will there be surprises along the way that will require major or minor changes in the overall book? Will there be sidetracks I'll find interesting and break out of the outline to follow? Will there be things I thought would happen that, when I get there, no longer make sense?

You bet yer ass!

But I would chance to say that there are writers who just start out and see where their character, story and imagination carry them. God bless 'em. I'm convinced they still are doing in their heads what I, at least when I was starting out, had to do on paper, but I can't write by the seat of my pants. I have to have as clear an idea as I can manage of at least the major plot points and who these characters are before I can start (much less finish) a novel.

And please…please don't tell me you just get it started and your characters take over and tell you what they want to do. That's just writerly bullshit…part of the "mystique" writers present about the writing process so it will appear more interesting than what the job really is…which is sitting your ass at a desk and trying to grind out the words. As someone—I forget who—once said: Writing is "putting the best word in the perfect place."

That's all it is. Honest. And no matter how you go about doing that after three or four of however many hundreds of pages you can type "The End," then you've done your job.

Side note: I didn't use a written outline for *The Cove*, the novel I recently completed. By the time you read this, I hope to have sold *The Cove*, but the marketplace is tougher than ever here in the year 2009. Is it any better when you're reading this? I fear not, and I'm afraid *The Cove* will be the trunk novel my heirs will discover after I'm gone and will publish to great acclaim, for all the goddamned good it will do me then. For the record, though, I had a very clear idea what the opening scene in the book would be, and what the last scene would be, but I had no idea what would be in the middle. So I just wrote the story. Since it was based on real characters and events that I knew personally from growing up on the Atlantic Coast and from talking to friends who live along the coast, I lived with this book bubbling inside my head so long that I "just wrote" it without outlining. It seemed to spill out of me, but at *no point* did I feel as though my characters were "taking over" and telling me what to do with the story. I was in control of the story all the way, and I decided what the characters would do or say. I just let it unwind.

Also, for the record, with the book I'm working on now—*Mockingbird Bay*—I outlined it using note cards, a different color card for each character's storyline. I even wrote brief character sketches for each of the main characters.

I hope some of this helps or at least explains why I write the way I write, but I realize this is not the "autobiography" I'm supposed to be writing, so I'll see if I can get this choo-choo back on track.

Chapter 17

"Are We Still in the Doldrums?"

So after my mother died, I quit writing for a year and tried to get my head together. And then Rich Chizmar, Ginjer Buchanan, and Chris Golden threw me lifelines. I know we were friends. But I'm not sure they realize to this day how grateful I am for what they did. I'm not sure they realize just how close to the edge I was.

And then I got divorced.

I joke now that if I'm ever going to get married again, I'll just find a woman I hate and give her a house and a car. The truth was, I stayed in my marriage longer than I should have, but I'm glad I did simply because of the three amazing sons I have as a result of that marriage. All of my sons are creative, compassionate, good people. Sure, like all kids, they gave their mother and me a run for the money when they were young, but—somehow—even as the marriage was spiraling out of control, they came through better people. I find it interesting that two of my three sons work in health care/social work related jobs, taking care of the unfortunate and the mentally challenged.

(Now that I think of it, maybe they got their start living with a father like me.)

My children helped me keep it together, too, of course. They were what I was living for at the absolute worst, when my career was washing up in broken pieces on the shore and my marriage had become a bed of nails.

But friends—old and new—helped turn me around and

usher me into what I see now is the second act of my writing career.

I've already mentioned this, but let's nail it down. When I started out, the only flesh and blood writer I knew (other than the handful of professors and students I knew in college who wrote poetry and "precious reminiscences" parading as real stories) was Steve King. And I spent a good deal of mental energy, wishing and thinking and hoping I could gain at least a modicum of that level of fortune and fame. When it looked like *Nightstone* would get me there, and then things collapsed, I knew I had to readjust. My only fear was that I would be forced to take a full-time day job that would finish killing off my already snuffed spirit.

When this happens—and if you're in the writing business long enough, it will happen—you have to reinvent yourself. Look at Madonna...or the Beatles...or Prince... or Steve King. What do they have in common?

Like sharks, they never stopped moving. They continually did the one thing you have to do to survive. They continually challenged themselves creatively. They didn't keep repeating past performances to the point of self-parody. They didn't rest. They evolved. Sometimes it worked. Sometimes it didn't. But they didn't stop. They kept pushing ahead. And with those (and so many other) examples in front of me, I knew I had to write, so what was I going to write?

Well, like I said, I always did like writing short stories, and some of them were challenging, but mostly my short stories were 1) a response to a specific request for a story, and 2) a way to make a quick buck, and 3) a way to experiment with different voices and styles and ways of telling a story...experiments that I sometimes used in subsequent novels.

Those are all good reasons to write short stories (except for reason 2. The money for short stories is seldom good…unless you happen to have a story in an anthology with a Stephen King story. Then, for some reason, the royalty check suddenly looks damned good!).

This brings me to a point I often make and which is, I think, important.

The conventional wisdom, at least the way I received it in college and afterwards, seems to be that you start writing short stories as "warm-ups"…as a testing ground… all in preparation for when you start to write "THE NOVEL." It's like there is this false hierarchy, that you can't even approach a novel until you've cut your teeth, so to speak, on short stories. The analogy may be that you have to crawl before you can walk, and only then can you run.

I'm nothing if not the exception that proves the rule.

I had dabbled a little while with short stories, but I hadn't really sat down and honed the craft before I started my first (published) novel. I didn't have the ideas popping in my head. Writers like Matt Costello and Chris Golden irritate the shit out of me because they're *so* good at something I am *so* bad at. Getting ideas. I used to say in interviews that I only get one idea a year, so I make sure it's enough for a whole novel. Like the old saying goes: "When an idea gets into an empty head, it has a hell of a time."

The truth is, I had two novels published (*Moondeath* and *Moonbog*) and one more under contract (*Nightstone*) before I sold my first story. And only then, I sold the story because an editor (Charles Waugh, who lived in Maine and worked with

Isaac Asimov on numerous anthologies), called and asked me for a story.

I was, of course, flattered and intimidated.

I had always admired Asimov (along with the heroes of real science fiction: Clarke, Heinlein, Sturgeon, Herbert, *et al*) and you can bet your ass I wanted to be in that anthology. The anthology had a theme, which immediately helped me focus my imagination. They wanted a "deal with the devil" story.

Easy enough.

But I sure as hell didn't want to regurgitate another Faust story, so I racked my brain (a short rack, I hear some of you say) and I came up with "Colt .24," a story that involved a gun that when you fired it, the bullet wouldn't hit the target until twenty-four hours later. The plot involved a guy who, in order to prove the gun is harmless, puts it to his head and pulls the trigger. Only after that does he learn about the twenty-four hour delay, and he's desperately waiting for the bullet to hit.

Cool idea, I thought, and so did Charles Waugh. I thought I was going to pass out when he told me that Asimov chose the final entries. A high point: having a word of validation (and a check!) from Isaac Asimov. I met the Good Doctor years later at the World Science Fiction Convention when it was in Boston (the year I couldn't afford a room and slept in the theatre during the all-night movies). He was a genuinely funny and engaging man, and I wish I had known him better. But we orbited different stars, he and I, like a lot of writers I admire and am nervous about approaching.

So after that sale, I adopted the practice of not writing a short story unless or until someone asked me for one. I certainly didn't do this out of any sense of ego. Quite the opposite. I did it because I didn't want to experience what every writer experiences—*rejection*! I had enough of a crisis of confidence, trying to write a novel a year (which is about what I averaged for a while). Writing a story and submitting it blind and then having it rejected would be just too much to bear. So, to this day, I have rarely (if ever? I'm honestly not sure) submitted a story "over the transom," as they say.

But other editors did ask me for stories from time to time, and I complied. I can think of only one time an editor asked for a story from me and then turned down what I sent in, but he was (and is) an asshole.

I worked with most of the best editors in the horror business and a few of the lousy ones. I had good experiences and bad. Some stories were edited so heavily I barely recognized my work, while some were set to print exactly as I wrote them, typos and all. After a while, I was surprised to see that I had enough short stories for a collection, so I approached Rich Chizmar about that. Part of my sailing out of the doldrums was what happened with *Bedbugs*, my first short story collection.

Side note: As of this writing, I am still waiting to see *Occasional Demons*, my second short story collection. I hope you have a copy by the time you read this because that book has been "at the printers" for a helluva long time.

Chapter 18

"Tattooed Soap Opera Watching Motorcycle Riding Psychopathic Artist"

I had the stories selected for *Bedbugs* when I met someone who, when you first meet him, seems to fit the title of this chapter to a T.

His name is Glenn Chadbourne, and if you're a NECon regular—even if you've only been once—you know Glenn. You see, when *Bedbugs* started coming together, I was working at Borders (I had a family to support). One of my co-workers, a friendly fellow named Ralph Jesse—we called him "Jesse"— said he knew "this artist guy" who said he was a huge fan of mine. Would I like to meet him?

I said, "Sure," while thinking—Jesus, what have I gotten myself into this time?

That thought was reinforced when Jesse's friend arrived. If you know Glenn, you know what I mean. On first sight, Glenn is scary. He looks like he could just as easily rip your arms off and flail you to death with them as give you the time of day. Glenn is big in every way, but most of all in two things: his art and his heart.

In spite of his big, bad, biker looks, Glenn is a pussycat, and I don't care if he's mad at me for saying so. He is kind and generous to a fault, and his artwork…well, just look at the work he did for *Bedbugs* or Steve's *Secretary of Dreams* (Vols. 1 and 2). Glenn and I hit it off immediately, and I asked him to show me some of his art the next time we got together. Well, about a week or two later, he showed up at the store with a huge pen and ink drawing—the one that became the cover for the Cemetery Dance edition of *Bedbugs*. (There was a paperback edition from Leisure Books later, but honestly, the book is only half of what it should be because it doesn't have all of Glenn's artwork.)

I was amazed…stunned…impressed

I called Rich and asked if he had an artist in mind to do the illustrations for *Bedbugs*. He didn't, and I said: "Well, I think I found the guy." Rich said it was my book, my choice of artist, and although I doubt it would ever have come to that, I think I would have withdrawn the book if Rich had said I couldn't use Glenn's art.

Use it we did, and Rich was so impressed by Glenn's work that he has become a regular for all CD publications, books and magazines and "specials." And I'm happy to see Glenn getting lots of work from other publishers who appreciate his unique style and execution.

As for the "Soap Opera Watching Motorcycle Riding Psychopathic Artist"—only the "psychopathic" part is a lie. The rest is true.

Chapter 19
"A Day in the Life"

Sometimes the transitions between these chapters are smooth; sometimes—like this one—they're abrupt. One reason for that is I didn't follow my own rule. I got so involved in writing the section on Glenn that I finished it and then stopped for the day, more than satisfied that I had written around 3,500 words.

Problem is, I ended the day's work by ending a section, and there's no organic flow to the next topic.

So I'll jump right to it and say this section is going to be about my typical day.

Who'd be interested in that? I hear you ask.

Who, indeed?

Writing this piece has been challenging, and I see by my handy-dandy word count that I'm still only about two-thirds finished. But the "writing life," while perhaps glamorous, is certainly not exciting. Well, I suppose if you make gazillions of dollars and can travel and take time off, it's glamorous, but for most writers, writing is more than a job; it's an obsession. Like John Irving said (in one of his books or in an interview, maybe): "You have to get obsessed and stay obsessed."

Sadly, that's true.

To survive the ups and downs of this crazy business, you have to be more than dedicated. You have to be insane! Well, maybe not insane, but it would help.

For a brief mental exercise, try this: Imagine what you would do with your life if you didn't write.

You imagining?

Not so pretty, is it?

So writers write, and that's it, but I have met two types of writers. I know people who love to write. They may not enjoy every aspect of the process (pre-writing, writing the first draft, revising the second and subsequent drafts, editing, and sending it out and waiting for a response from an editor), but they love the act of creating, of—as I often say—"sitting at my desk and making up goofy shit."

I'm one of those kinds of writers. I struggle sometimes, especially at the beginning of a project, but I love losing myself in the writing of whatever it is I'm working on. Some parts of my brain shut down while others light up, and when I sit back and observe what I'm doing (trying not to "burst the bubble"), I realize I've been lost in the words and the story.

Then there are those writers who do not enjoy writing, but love having written. They don't like the process (for whatever reasons) and are only happy once they have something finished and can drop it in your lap.

I have no problem with those kinds of writers (although I do think they're more responsible for creating and reinforcing the "mystique" of writing). Bully for them! As long as they write something that works for their readers. But there are a few....I think the worst example of this type of writer is one who has a website (who doesn't?) where he/she (no, I won't tell you who this is in case my perception of him/her is wrong) posts one or more notices each hour on his/her progress...how many words he/she has written that day.

What bullshit, if I may be so bold.

Who gives a sweet shit about how many words you've squeezed out today?

Who gives a flying fuck how many words you had to delete?

Does this writer *really* think readers care *that* much about the daily excretion of words?

What utter nonsense!

In the end, what matters is how good the story is. Like I said—I value story (plot, character and setting) over style (tone, mood and syntax) any and every day.

If you don't agree with me, fine. I got no beef with you, but there's a good chance I wouldn't be interested in what you write. But this noodges forward the question some of you may have: What is my "typical day" of writing? So here it is:

I usually wake up between 9:00 or 9:30 and lurch out of bed by 10:00. Without eating breakfast, I stagger over to the desk (morning comes like a cement block to the head for me) and check my emails and the daily rants on Shocklines. The important emails are usually from the previous afternoon, but I generally only check my emails this one time, in the morning. Email and websites take an hour or two, and then around 12:00—no later than 1:00—I head into the kitchen and have "breakfast."

After breakfast, which is usually a glass of OJ and a slice of whole wheat bread with natural peanut butter—none of that "brown lard" for me, sometime around noon, I head into the living room, power up the old laptop, sit in the Morris chair and start writing.

As you now know, it doesn't matter how long I sit there. As soon as I hit over two thousand words for the day, I consider my work done for the day. I'm almost always done by 3:00, but some days I have to sit there until 4:00 or 5:00. Not often though, so once I hit my word count, it's out to the deck to have a cigar and read for an hour or so. On crappy days (rain, ice, snow or fog) I forego the cigar and read on the couch.

Around 4:30, Holly gets home from work, and we walk *her* dogs and then have supper. The dishes are usually done by 6:30, so we watch our usual weekday TV (*NBC Nightly News, The Daily Show, The Colbert Report,* and *Countdown with Keith Olbermann*). Holly gets up early for work, so she trundles off to bed after "Keithie," and I either watch a movie or read until somewhere between midnight and two in the morning. On rare occasions, I'll write at night, but not usually. And then I'm off to bed to start the whole thing over again.

Sounds exciting, huh?

Don't you wish you were me?

For fuck's sake—no, you don't.

I lost track of the days. I don't "enjoy" the seasons—and believe me, here in Maine, we get *seasons.* But they all blend together because the only important part of my day is when I'm writing. That's what I live for…getting lost in the story and characters, and trying to make coherent sense of it all.

I didn't mention what happens when I sleep, but I will now. I'm talking about dreams. I mentioned how my mother helped me understand the importance of dreams when I was young, and I have an active dream life. I mean, night after night, I get the weirdest, most lucid, most frightening, most confusing dreams you can imagine. And here's how I do it.

I have a technique I'm going to share with you. I don't know how or when I discovered it, but if you want vivid dreams, try this. Don't eat anything after supper, and then, on an empty stomach, just before you go to bed, eat a banana. The banana doesn't have to be green, but the fresher the better. An almost rotten banana doesn't have the same kick.

I guarantee you will get wild dreams, and if (like me) you enjoy an active dream life, you'll thank me later. If you're afraid of nightmares—and don't see them as source material for stories—then don't try this.

A tuna fish sandwich will have the same effect, but it's more calories, so you may not want to go that route. Don't ask me why or how this works. It obviously has to be some chemical(s) in the banana and tuna fish.

Try it...and sweet dreams!

Chapter 20
"Return to the Twilight Zone"

I think I've made it clear that I wasn't a good student, either in high school or college. I think I went on for my Master's in English because there was nothing else to do. I always think about that line the Dan Aykroyd character says in the first Ghostbusters movie when they get kicked out of the university. His line is something like "I've worked in the private sector. They expect results."

I think that was my thinking. I stayed in academia because it was "safe" and you could just, like, read and write (and teach) and not have to deal with the real world.

And when you think about it, isn't that what writers want?

We all live in our heads, imagining the craziest shit—and even crazier—wanting someone to pay us to do that!

My sister went to Uppsala College, in East Orange, New Jersey, (now defunct) and my brother went to Springfield College (now surrounded by security fences topped with razor wire). I went to a state university. And I was so dense that, even though several of my high-achieving friends from high school also went to private colleges, they were outside of my ken. I never even considered that I could possibly attend a "good" school. I made do with the University of Maine. It was much cheaper, for one, but money wasn't the only or even first issue; it was my level of intellect. In the end, I think UMaine Orono was a good fit for me because I left there with a BA and MA in English, feeling as though a lot of doors had opened for me.

When it came time for my own children to go to college, I—of course—wanted them to have what I couldn't have—a great education and a great school. Now Aaron, the oldest, wasn't academically inclined. He was—and is—an amazing musician who I honestly think is going to make an impact on the "music scene" in Austin, Texas. Time will tell. But Jesse had the great fortune to go to Clark University in Worcester, Massachusetts, and Matti attended Ithaca College in New York. I think (hope—because of what those four years cost) that they got all they could from college and then some.

But I always felt like I was on the outside looking in.

One of my very best friends—Bob Stone—went to Dartmouth. I clearly remember being jealous that he had such an opportunity...even though I had to privately acknowledge that I never could have been accepted at a school like Dartmouth (or Clark, or Ithaca) and even if I had, I would have flunked out cold.

I'm not that smart, intellectually. That doesn't mean I think I'm "stoopit." Far from it. I read history, science, biography, as well as fiction, and I think I know more than the average American (which, now that I think about it, isn't saying much when you consider something like 18% of Americans still think the sun revolves around the earth). And what I lack in "left brain" functions, I think I more than make up for with "right brain" functions.

Who's to say?

But I'm trying to bring this around to a discussion of Ithaca College. Don't get me wrong. I was impressed by Clark, and I think Jesse got a top-notch education there, but I would have *loved* to have had an opportunity to go to a school like Ithaca. It would have been the perfect match for me when I was a student. Even better, the years I would have been there was the same time Rod Serling was teaching there.

Imagine that!

To have a writing class with *Rod Serling* as your *instructor*!

(FYI: I just did a word count for the day's work. The writing hasn't been coming easily today. I don't know why. But I was stunned to see that I am still exactly 22 words shy of 2,000 words for the day. I'm not counting this little aside as part of my daily word count, so I have to churn out one or two more sentences before I'll call it a day. Maybe the magic will return tomorrow, because, like "Old Lodge Skins"—Chief Dan George—said in one of my all-time favorite movies, *Little Big Man*—"Some days the magic works and some days it doesn't.")

We took Jesse out to Ithaca to check out IC and Cornell when he was applying to schools, and I immediately fell in love with the area. I don't know why. If you believe in reincarnation (I don't), then maybe it was a "past life" thing. I have no idea why the town and college and lake and whole area appealed to me so strongly, but it did.

When it was Matti's turn to apply to schools, he put almost all of his effort into applying to schools in England, Wales and Scotland. He even got accepted (but no financial aid, dammit!) into St. Andrews, but because of finances he only had one college—Ithaca—in the States as his one and only safety school.

And that's where he went.

I was happy for him and tried—like any good parent—not to live out my dream through my kids. I wanted him to find his own way, and I hoped Ithaca would be as good a fit for him as I imagined it would have been for me. (Although, to be honest,

I went to school before personal computers, the Internet, and cell phones, so I might have felt as isolated from civilization in Ithaca, New York, as I did in Orono, Maine).

At the end of Matti's spring semester freshman year, I was dreading having to drive out there to get him and his stuff. It's a seven- or eight-hour drive each way. And I feared I would have to rent a van to get all his stuff. But, lo and behold, the college announced that they were having a Rod Serling Conference! This would occur about two or three weeks before the end of the semester, so I saw this as an opportunity to drive out there in my small Hyundai Accent, see Matti, bring back a lot of his stuff, and attend the conference. I would get Matti and the rest of his stuff later.

So I went to the first Rod Serling conference, and had a good time. I'd never been to an honest-to-Gosh "academic conference" before. NECon doesn't count. You're supposed to laugh at that. I have to tell you, I was amazed by the event, and there were several high points. Old films of Serling teaching...screenings of long-lost films...and Rod's wife, Carol, was there.

I wanted to meet Carol and say something that would, no doubt, have been eminently stupid, like: "I really enjoyed your husband's writing." And—to be honest—I didn't know quite how to approach her. I mean, her husband had been dead about thirty years, so she wasn't exactly in mourning, but because the conference was to honor Serling and his work, there was a high level of respect and...yes, of wondering what else Serling might have written had he not died so young.

So on the first day of the conference, there was Carol Serling, talking to people, and there was me, experiencing a full-throttle turd in the punchbowl moment. I didn't belong here.

I could never have gotten accepted into a school like Ithaca. I could never have survived, and here were all these—as we say in Maine—"wicked smart" people.

I noticed this one young man who approached Carol and began chatting with her. I noticed his confidence and the ease with which he talked and laughed with her, and I assumed they were friends. I watched, wishing I had the *cojones* to speak with her too…but I didn't.

When this young man was through talking with Carol, he and I and everyone else were sort of milling around, waiting for something to happen. They guy I had noticed talking to Carol drifted past me, and he noticed my nametag. (Yes. Uncharacteristically, I was wearing a nametag.) He stopped in his tracks and said something like "Are you *the* Rick Hautala?"

Now in instances like that, I always wish I had the balls to say something wiseass, like "Who wants to know?" or "Maybe."

I didn't go wiseass this time; I said something eloquent like, "Uhhh, yeah."

He introduced himself, and we shook hands, and that's how I first met Mark Steensland. Since that fateful encounter (it must have been 2006), Mark and I have written, and he's produced and directed, several films, including *Lovecraft's Pillow*, *Dead@17*, *Peekers*, *The Ugly File*, and *Graffito*, and there are more short films and features to come.

Chapter 21
"Things Get Mushy"

Of course, meeting Mark was important to me because this was the moment when I began to redefine myself and my writing. You, see, up to around this point, I still had a feeling of…I'm not quite sure how to express it, but a feeling of protectiveness and …is "priority" the word I'm looking for?

I'm not sure.

But throughout my early, and, I guess we have to say mid-career, I was driven to write books and I felt protective of them. They were my babies, and when a book gets published, it's a lot like sending a child of yours off to college…out into the "big, bad world" where they will sink or swim on their own devices, and there's little if anything you can do about it. Continuing my already twisted metaphor, I was a "helicopter parent" for my books, but then I finally got to the point where I realized I was being foolish.

Look, you write the best book you can…you pour everything you have into it…but then it goes out into the world, where editors and publicity and promotion people and salespeople and customers make decisions over which you have absolutely no control.

You get that?

Because I didn't.

True to form, I took things "too personally," as friends and teachers and family members have said to me since I was a little kid. I was miserable once a book came out because I believed whatever bad reviews the book (or story) got, and I didn't believe the good reviews or when someone recognized me and said how much they loved my books. (That happened just yesterday. I had given Holly a check to deposit, and when the teller saw and recognized my name, she told Holly how much she *loved* my books and asked when something new was coming out.)

The fact that I didn't dare approach Carol Serling was indicative of how I feel most (read: "all") of the time.

I may laugh with friends, and I may tell jokes, and I may hang out some with friends, but I am basically Scandinavian and all that implies. (Remember the "looking at *your* shoes" joke? It's true!) So when I see someone I would like to meet, I usually don't go over and introduce myself. I let the chance go by because I convince myself that person wouldn't want to meet me anyway.

That happened in a big way in—I'll never forget this year— 2001 because that's the year—at NECon—where I met Holly Newstein and pretty much flipped over her at first sight.

It's no secret. A lot of people at NECon are debauched. We go there to drink and party and laugh and talk, and if we're really, really lucky—get laid. Not everyone is lucky, and I certainly wasn't because I behaved myself at NECon. I was married, even though in the late '90s my marriage was in name only, and I was basically shy.

So when I first saw Holly, I didn't know what to do.

We started chatting. I "arranged" things so I was in her vicinity as often as possible. I even gave up playing in the softball game. I had recently had surgery, and that was a great excuse to play croquet that summer, and I finagled it so Holly and I played together. Of course, when I learned she was married and had two kids, I was crushed, and I knew there was no hope—for me—anyway.

Then we started emailing each other, and I quickly learned that her marriage was on the rocks, too.

A ray of hope, however slim.

That October (2001) I moved out of the house and got an apartment. I kept e-mailing Holly, and when I learned things were at a breaking point in her marriage, I boldly (some would say "stupidly", some would say "romantically") told her she could stay with me if she needed a place to get away.

Two weeks later, she moved in, and while I'm old enough and cynical enough not to put all my faith into the idea of "soul mates" and "eternal love," I did find the person who I consider the "love of my life." We've been together for eight years now, and if it wasn't for NECon (and a little white lie Roman Ranieri told me), I never would have met Holly and been as happy (as happy as a Finn can get, anyway) as I am today.

So that's it for the "mushy" part.

Holly and I aren't the only couple who met at NECon—Beth Massie and Cortney Skinner, Craig Shaw Gardner and his wife Barbara, Tom Monteleone and Dickle—and slews of other "NECon couples."

Like Virginia, NECon is for lovers.

But the other point I'm trying to make here is something that I may have finally come around to only because I'm getting old and because I've been doing this "writing thang" long enough now.

Writing *isn't* revealing your heart and soul to everyone who reads you.

It *isn't* like having a child that you have to protect, nurture and support.

It's just a fucking story!

It may be good; it may suck; and it probably is just "all right."

In all likelihood, it won't change the course of literature and it won't have an impact that lasts much beyond what you do with the money (however large or small) you were paid for the story.

In other words: Don't take yourself so seriously.

If what you've written has flaws (and everything does. I defy you to name a "perfect" piece of literature. Hell, even *Hamlet* has flaws!), go on and write something else. Learn from your mistakes. Do better the next time, knowing that your writing will not be a steadily rising curve. You will have successes and failures, and more often than not, what succeeds and when it succeeds will probably have nothing to do with you.

And if you find yourself at a standstill, then reinvent yourself.

For years, I'd been struggling to write screenplays, and the strongest reaction I got was from one producer who told me the screenplay I'd written based on my novel *The Mountain King* had "best stay in your desk drawer." But I kept at it because 1) writing screenplays was fun and not nearly as labor-intensive as a novel, 2) there was, in general, better money selling a screenplay than a novel, and 3) someday I want to see a feature film flash the credit "Screenplay by Rick Hautala"…it will be even better if the movie is a hit!

You gotta dream, right?

After all, writing is basically dreaming with your eyes open.

Isn't it?

That's how I feel, anyway. I'd love to have my brain hooked up to a machine that measures brainwaves while I'm writing. I bet the pattern would be close to if not identical to the brainwave pattern of when I'm asleep and dreaming.

So meeting Mark and "reinventing" myself and meeting Holly and finding—again—my faith that there is still love in this world are the two key turning points at what I insist on calling the "midpoint" of my career.

Like I said earlier, there were a handful of Texians when I fought at the Alamo, but Holly and Mark were with me at San Jacinto.

Chapter 22
"Where Do We Go from Here?"

I don't live an interesting life.

I have good friends, people I know I can count on. I also have numerous acquaintances...people I know mostly from writing who, while friendly, aren't the people I would trust with my bank PIN number. And—yes , I have some people I don't like and even a few I consider enemies (if that's not too strong a word).

But most of my life, I live inside my head. I read a lot. I write as much as I can because I realize now that I have more ideas for stories than I can possibly live to tell. I watch movies and some TV. And I love blizzards when I can sit on the couch, read, and watch the snow pile up. Holly would rather live further south than Maine, but maybe it's my heritage as a Finn that keeps me here. I love the cold weather.

Christ, this is starting to sound like a "I love poetry and taking a walk in the rain" pitch on a singles network. Sorry.

But in trying to think of something—anything—amazing or interesting or amusing that happened to me, I come up dry.

Maybe all the adventure in my life happened in my head. I was encouraged by my mother to put a value on dreams, but I think maybe I should have "lived" more. After all, they tell aspiring writers to "write what you know."

Side note: That's stupid advice! How can you restrict yourself to what you know...unless what you dream and imagine comes under that umbrella. Writing only what you know would lead to a lot of bullshit writing about English Literature grad students who haven't done *anything* in their lives. Come to think of it—that's why I don't read a lot of what's redundantly called "literary fiction."

Perhaps a life of the mind isn't such a good thing. Maybe a "life" is what I need. Like Stan Wiater says, "Some people have a life. We have NECon." But so much of life—for me, anyway—has been the emotions and feelings and thoughts and—yes, even dreams that happen, not the superficial detail of what I did.

Okay, sure...I flew to Helsinki, Finland, to promote a book of mine (*Cold Whisper*, which was translated into Finnish as *Haamu*) that was published there. The book even made the Finnish Best-Sellers list, so I can call myself an international bestselling author. I went to one of the HWA meetings in Redondo Beach, California, and some things happened there that might make for an amusing story or two, but the statute of limitations hasn't run out yet on some of them. And a few years ago, Holly and I went to St. Kitts and had a marvelous week, sitting on the beach and drinking Carib beer as the sun sank into the Caribbean. I still have a fantasy of making enough money from books or movies so we can buy a summer camp here in Maine and have a condo or small house in St. Kitts for the winter.

But none of those events are "story-worthy." I'm not like my buddy Tom Monteleone, who can spin silver threads from the seemingly mundane—and not-so-mundane!—things that happen to him. What I do is write stories. I like to sit in my office and make up goofy shit, and I hope and pray I continue to get paid to do that.

Look, folks, I've already passed my 2,000 words for the day, and I'm going to break my rule (again) and stop writing at the end of a chapter. I hope when I pick this up tomorrow, I'll have more to say about something because—to be honest—I'm running out of gas, and I still have about five thousand more words to write before I finish this project.

Chapter 23

"Ghosts in the Machine"

I was lucky to "come of age" in the late Fifties and Sixties.

When I read Ray Bradbury and saw *Twilight Zone* episodes like "Walking Distance," even when I was young, I felt a yearning nostalgia for times and places, people and things that have already passed. Of course, that feeling was also expressed in my interest in ancient civilizations and mythology, but that tied in more with dreams than reality. I felt a genuine yearning for my youth slipping away, even when I was a youth.

Strange, huh?

Bummer, too.

But even as a young child, I was sad—and terrified—that life passes by.

I remember one day in the winter, I couldn't have been more than ten years old. My friends and I were sliding on the hill behind my grandfather's house. It was a beautiful winter day after a fresh snowfall. The sky was a bright blue that hurt your eyes to look at. The snow was fresh and white as we carved new tracks down the hill with our sleds.

It was glorious!

And as I was trudging up the hill, dragging my sled, I watched as two of my friends—Ray Makkonen and Jimmy Wayrenen—more Finns—came sliding down, laughing and whooping it up. And as I watched them, I had a single, terrifying thought. I watched my friends and suddenly felt a jolt. It hit at the deepest core of my being when I thought: "Damn…

someday we'll all be dead."

Think about that for a minute.

If you're also a writer or reader of "horror," you must recognize this thought because you've had it yourself, in a different context. This is the one thing that binds readers and writers of horror. We are aware of the horror of death…the emptiness of non-existence. And we write stories that defy the notion that death ends it all.

What's a vampire, if not proof that there is survival of some sort after death?

A zombie? A ghost? The Mummy?

All symbolize the same thing…our hope that—somehow—we will survive death, and the soul-chilling fear that we won't. That when we're gone, we're so fucking gone we won't even know we're gone. Personal annihilation.

So there I was, a little kid no more than ten years old getting a blast of mortality much colder than any winter wind. Like the spot where I first read *The Martian Chronicles*, I could take you to the hill and show you the exact spot I was standing when the thought hit me with all its mind-numbing, bone-chilling, terrifying power. Well, I could if my father hadn't sold the land and there wasn't a house on that hill now.

But you get the point.

I was living a seemingly normal, perfectly fine little life, but in my heart…in my soul, I was wrestling with demons, and I had no one to talk to about them. I never confessed my deepest inner fears to parents, friends, or loved ones. I lived with them, and I think that's what eventually directed (you might say "drove") me to write the stories I write.

So why ghost stories?

I have no idea other than to speculate that, on some level, I feel a deep measure of guilt and remorse for things and times past, for people lost and deeds undone, or deeds that never should have been done.

I feel a nostalgic longing for "possibilities" that will remain just that—mere possibilities that will *never* come to fruition no matter how hard we work and wish for them.

Growing up is never easy. Wasn't it Mark Twain who said something about how writers don't have to suffer to write because adolescence is suffering enough for anyone?

So why do I feel "guilty"?

What did I do?

I have dreams—nightmares—where, when I was young I killed someone and hid it—even from myself, and, in my dream, I "discover" the body and the sin and the guilt. In fact it's been close to fifty years since I killed anything. (Well, other than that damned woodchuck that was cleaning out my rows of beans one summer. No Hav-A-Heart trap for me. That bastard got what I call "lead poisoning" and did a nice little bit of breakdancing before he died.) Before that, the last living creature I killed was a chickadee I shot with a friend's rifle. Talk about "sanctioning with extreme prejudice!" The poor little sucker was just sitting there on a branch, minding his own bird business, and I leveled my friend's shotgun at him and gave him a ride on the "Lead Ball Express."

And then I cried.

There I was with my friend, feeling like Peter of "Peter and The Wolf" with my little pop gun, and then I saw what *real* buckshot can do. I remember seeing a feather or two flutter to the ground, but that was all. That poor little bird was obliterated from existence *because of me*!

I could not accept that I had actually terminated a life, and I have seldom fired a gun since, and never at another living being (except for that pesky woodchuck), but even he didn't really "have it comin'," as they say.

Do I believe in ghosts?

Well, like I say about most things paranormal, "I don't believe it and I never want to see it."

I have never seen a ghost. When I used to do book signings, now and then I'd get invited by a fan to "see" or "hear" the ghost at their houses. Some of them even brought photos to prove they had a ghost, but I've never gone when I've been invited. Like I said, I don't believe in ghosts and I don't want to see one.

The reason I say that is simple: I would, first and foremost, be suspicious that I was being set up. Maybe not maliciously, but an edge of paranoia usually (dare I say "always?") creeps in whenever I deal with "true believers."

What draws me to horror are the indefinable…the mysterious…the things you catch in the corner of your eye but which aren't there when you turn your head and look…the things (whatever they are) at the fringe of our awareness. I've been "aware" of them since I was little, and now—as a writer—I guess I try to recreate for myself, and hopefully for the reader, that wonderful, terrifying *frisson*.

I'm not much interested in bloodsucking or brain-eating or savage mutilation. Sometimes I am—especially when an editor contacts me and asks for, say, a story about "lesbian nuns who turn into werewolves." Then, sure, I'll see if the suggestion flares up in my imagination, but the natural tendency of my mind is toward the creepy...the spooky...the *truly* unknown.

So for these and whatever reasons are buried in my subconscious, it's primarily ghost stories for me.

Chapter 24
"Crawlspaces"

What I'm talking about (again) is childhood and the nostalgia for the past.

Like I said at the start of this, I had a perfectly normal-to-all-appearances childhood…the usual ups and downs….the triumphs and tragedies (all of them minor in the greater scheme of things)…the hopes and failures. Where things went weird was inside my head, and I think the Sixties expressed that this wasn't happening to just me, not with all the sex, drugs, and rock 'n roll, and the genuine concern we (and by "we" I mean "my gen-gen-gen-generation") was in a death spiral.

I think it still is. Not to wander into politics here, but I believe that if conservatives like Richard Nixon and Barry Goldwater were alive today, they'd be branded as "liberals" and thrown out of the Republican Party as it exists today. And for the record: Yes, I am a social liberal and a fiscal conservative, and I am worried by the extremes of both parties.

But I don't want to wander into politics. In these last few pages, I want to wander—or at least look into—the crawlspaces in my mind…because *that's* where true horror originates and where it resonates.

That image of a crawlspace is a key one from my childhood. The second house we lived in—the one my father built and five-year-old me helped (in my own feeble way) mix cement for the foundation and pound a few nails—the bedrooms at either end of the house had built-in bureaus that opened up into a narrow crawlspace that ran the length of the house. I used to hide in there and, on rainy days, even dare—with a flashlight, of course—to go some of the distance down from what was the bedroom my brother and I shared to my sister's bedroom.

The problem was the bathroom between the two bedrooms...and the pipes that blocked the way about halfway down. I wanted so much to be the first—and only—one of us kids to make it all the way down, but I was terrified that I would get stuck between the pipes and the inner wall...and my parents wouldn't be able to get me out...that they might not even hear my cries...and I would die there and molder away like a dead rat, trapped between the walls.

That was on the western side of the house; the eastern side also had "unused" space, but there was more of it. From my bedroom, in the wall right beside my bed, there was a small doorway—a hatch, almost, leading into an uninsulated attic. There was a main room, but like the crawlspace on the west, all there was, was a narrow passage, and at the end of each passage, a room about the size of a small closet.

Now why these spaces weren't incorporated into the living space of the house was always a mystery to me. Maybe it had something to do with insulation, because these spaces were filled with vermiculite, an insulating material that, I'm sure, will eventually kill me of lung cancer because of my exposure to it as a child. Exposure? Hell, we used to play in those "hidden" rooms all the time, and when I got a little older, it's where I hid my copies of *Playboy*, figuring my mother and father would never venture down there. Apparently they never did, because I never got busted, and the magazines...Fuck, there are probably a few copies still there, jammed under a floorboard like hidden treasure in a Hardy Boys book.

But I would have dreams about these crawlspaces. Of course, in the dreams, they're often distorted and trans-located, but to me they …somehow…represent the subconscious mind.

It wouldn't be the "subconscious" if we were "conscious" of it, now …would it?

But this is where …well, I was about to say "all writers" but I don't think everyone who writes is as aware of the subconscious mind as, say, horror writers are.

Because that is what we do.

We go into dark places…and narrow crawlspaces (what's narrower than a coffin?)…and we poke around…and we try, to the best of our limited ability, to bring some of these things out into the light. The problem is, sometimes, once we stir them up, they get away from us and cause havoc…and—even worse— they turn back on *us!* Their *liberators!*

Tell me, how is that fair?

We, the intrepid explorers of the subconscious and in some cases, the unconscious mind, sometimes end up doing more harm than good.

Sometimes.

But not always.

I am a firm believer that it's much better (and more "human") to explore…at least the fringes of darkness because it's better than sunshine and denial that dark spaces…crawl-spaces in the mind…exist. Of course, there is always the danger that the darkness will swallow you—

(Seriously. There are no guarantees…no guaranteed safe passage.)

—or that you will unleash something over which you have no control.

But that's life, ain't it?

I mean—ask yourself—honestly—what is there in this world that you *really* can control?

Maybe the microwave and, if you're lucky and smart, the TV remote and TIVO, but life—to me anyway, from the perspective of sixty years living with terror always somewhere nearby, gnawing at my mind and nerves—is a series of learning how to embrace and how to let go. Your romances...your friends, and worse, your children...your youth and vigor...your possessions...your health, and in some sad cases, your sanity—they all go away, sooner or later, and the measure of who and what we are as a species and as individuals is how well we handle these changes and losses, because as horror writers and readers, we all know what's waiting for us in the end.

Oblivion.

Christ, this is sounding more like a self-help book than an "autobiography" of a horror writer. And believe me, I do feel bad about not being able to impress you with a life lived full of adventure and intrigue. But I'm "just" a writer. I spend most of my time (and I'm most comfortable when I'm) *inside my own head.*

Friends and lovers have told me over the years that my attitude is egocentric, selfish, childish and all sorts of other "bad" things, but all of us are in the hands of fate when it comes to when and where we are born, and we're slaves to genetics and upbringing when it comes to how we flourish (or not) and what we make of it.

One thing that bothers me deeply is my observation (and

I hope I'm not engaging too much in what psychologists call "projection") is the number of people I see today who do not take personal responsibility for who they are and what they do. If they're not "adult children of alcoholics" or "victims of abuse," it has something to do with their past lives, or some such nonsense.

You know what I say…and try (and all too often fail) to do is *fuckin' deal with it*! Like the logo on a T-shirt I have that reads: "Put on your big-girl panties and deal with it."

Words to live by…to aspire to. And in the end—yeah, I'm gonna wrap this up a few thousand words short. Sorry, but I ain't getting paid by the word (or at all, other than glory) for doing this.

I know, in the final analysis—well, I hope it's not final; I'd like to live long enough to check out my perspective when I'm eighty or ninety—if you've read what I've written here carefully and gotten it in spite of my possibly awkward and at times inaccurate phrasing, I've given you the best explanation I can possibly give to why I am the person I am and why I write what I write. (In case you missed it—I write primarily ghost stories… about guilt…and unfinished business…and traces of what was…and might have been…and never will be.)

Given what I've been given by God (however you may conceive "God" or genetics or upbringing or inborn personality traits), I can only conclude this by repeating the heading from the prologue:

"I 'Yam What I 'Yam."

I want to thank you if you've stuck with me throughout this tedious essay. I suspect not many of you have bothered to read it carefully. I know it hasn't been easy for you. It hasn't been easy for me, either. I picked off more than a few "psychic scabs." Some of them are even bleeding.

But that's okay.

No hard feelings.

As I like to say: "In the greater scheme of things, what does it really matter?"

Like my friend Matt Costello says: "We're in the Peter Pan business." Even at sixty years old, in so many ways I am still nothing more than an eight- or ten-year-old boy wrestling with demons in the dark, pressing walls of a crawlspace that seems to be closing in...either that, or like Alice, I'm getting larger...

The real question that paralyzes me with fear is: *What does any of it matter?*

And you know what?

I've come up with an answer that suits me, at least.

It's simple, really.

I think *what matters* is how we treat people, whether we know them or not, whether we like them or not. The Buddha is right: We are all One.

I think *what matters* is that we live our lives with one simple goal—that when we leave the world, it will be a better place for our having been in it. Leaving the world worse off is not acceptable. Even not making an impact on the world isn't good enough. You have to do what you can to make this world a *better* place.

My job as a writer is to try to make the world better by entertaining people. Readers are, after all, investing time and money into a book or story of mine. And maybe...just a little bit...I hope to enlighten people. Finally, I want to shine the small, feeble light of my imagination into the darkness and hope against hope that if there's anything there, it won't burst out and devour me, body and soul.

For myself, the answers I get and the things I do don't always match up to such lofty ambitions, but I do know I try, in my life *and* in my writing (and am all too aware of the failings) to show how on some level I think we are all are wounded and how much just feeling a hand reach out in the darkness....not a cold, dead, skeletal hand, but a warm hand of flesh and blood that squeezes your hand reassuringly...is all we ever need.

And I know—in my life—that's what I've gotten from my friends, lovers, and children, and it's what I've always tried to give.

I think that's all there is...

Postscript

Rick wrote this autobiography in the late summer and fall of 2009, unbeknownst to me. I found the manuscript, with his handwritten edits, among his papers after he died in March 2013. I searched his hard drive for the file, but, characteristically, he must have figured no one would ever want to read his life story and ruminations on the craft of writing, and deleted it. So I retyped it, with his edits, into what you have just read.

In the four years since he wrote this, *Occasional Demons* did see print, and several other books as well, including *Reunion*, *Four Octobers*, *Glimpses* and *The Wildman*. His final novel, *The Demon's Wife*, and a sci-fi collaboration with Matt Costello titled *Star Road* are forthcoming, as well as his YA novel *Mockingbird Bay*.

We got married in 2011, mainly because we realized our exes could file for our death benefits if we didn't. Our sons grew up and prospered. Aaron made a lot of good music in Austin, Texas, but got homesick and is back in Portland, Maine. His sons Jesse and Matti are doing well in their chosen careers, and his stepsons Colin and Andrew Newstein are also doing well. Colin works for a bank in Reading, Pennsylvania, and Andrew is bound for law school.

In 2012 Rick received the Lifetime Achievement Award from the HWA, which was the high point of his career. The recognition affected him deeply, even though he claimed he only got it because he "didn't have the decency to go away." We spent a wonderful four days in Salt Lake City, catching up with old friends including Alamo buddies Joe Lansdale and Rick McCammon, and making a host of new friends like Pete Giglio, Charles Day, and Henry and Holli Snider. He was surprised at the enthusiasm of the "younger generation" and amazed at what an influence he had been on them. Self-deprecating to the end, the HWA weekend gave him the confidence to take his writing in different directions. He wrote two historical screenplays, one based on Evelyn Nesbit and the original "crime of the century" when her husband Harry Thaw murdered the architect and pedophile Stanford White, and one based on the 1889 Johnstown Flood. Both have received praise and interest, but no offers of production yet. *The Demon's Wife* is a romantic and wryly comic tale, albeit with supernatural overtones, and *Star Road* is an old-style rockin' sci-fi story. To the very end, Rick was evolving and improving as a writer.

I hope you have enjoyed Rick's memoir, and if you are an aspiring writer, found it instructive. Rick always believed in sticking to the basics and just telling the story, without flourishes. All he wanted to do was entertain his readers, fans and friends. Dazzling them with bullshit or pulling rank was never his style. As he says, we are all in this together.

—Holly Newstein Hautala
May 2013

About the Author

Under his own name, Rick Hautala wrote close to thirty novels, including the million-copy best seller *Night Stone*, as well as *Winter Wake*, *The Mountain King*, and *Little Brothers*. He published three short story collections: *Bedbugs*, *Occasional Demons*, and *Glimpses: The Best Short Stories of Rick Hautala*. He had over sixty short stories published in a variety of national and international anthologies and magazines.

Writing as A. J. Matthews, his novels include the bestsellers *The White Room*, *Looking Glass*, *Follow*, and *Unbroken*.

His recent and forthcoming books include *Indian Summer*, a new "Little Brothers" novella, as well as two novels, *Chills* and *Waiting*. He recently sold *The Star Road*, a science fiction novel co-written with Matthew Costello, to Brendan Deneen at Thomas Dunne/St. Martin's.

With Mark Steensland, he wrote several short films, including the multiple award-winning *Peekers*, based on the short story by Kealan Patrick Burke; *The Ugly File*, based on the short story by Ed Gorman; and *Lovecraft's Pillow*, inspired by a suggestion from Stephen King.

Born and raised in Rockport, Massachusetts, Rick was a graduate of the University of Maine in Orono with a Master of Arts in English Literature. He lived in southern Maine and is survived by his wife, author Holly Newstein.

In 2012, he was awarded the Lifetime Achievement Award from the Horror Writers Association. For more information, check out his website www.rickhautala.com.

Curious about other Crossroad Press books?
Stop by our site:
http://store.crossroadpress.com
We offer quality writing
in digital, audio, and print formats.

Enter the code FIRSTBOOK
to get 20% off your first order from our store!
Stop by today!